Greenhill Books

ATTACK AIRCRAFT
AND BOMBERS OF THE WORLD

GREENHILL MILITARY MANUALS

The B-2 is the most capable of today's attack platforms USAF

ATTACK AIRCRAFT
AND BOMBERS OF THE WORLD

GREENHILL MILITARY MANUALS

Anil R. Pustam

Greenhill Books, London
Stackpole Books, Pennsylvania

Greenhill Books

This edition of *Attack Aircraft and Bombers of the World*
First published 2004 by Greenhill Books, Lionel Leventhal Limited, Park House, 1 Russell Gardens, London NW11 9NN
and
Stackpole Books, 5067 Ritter Road, Mechanicsburg, PA 17055, USA

British Library Cataloguing in Publication Data
Pustam, Anil
Attack aircraft
1. Attack planes
I. Title 623.7'463
ISBN 1-85367-581-4

Library of Congress Cataloging-in-Publication Data available

Designed by John Anastasio
Printed and Bound in Singapore

Front cover illustration: A Tornado GR4 of the RAF, able to undertake a wide range of attack missions

Contents

INTRODUCTION

The term "attack aircraft", particularly if bombers are included in the classification, encompasses an extremely wide range of types. At the bottom of the scale are turboprop trainers, normally simple machines which could be effective in counter-insurgency (COIN) and close air support (CAS) against less sophisticated adversaries. Some manufacturers have developed specialised attack derivatives of these aircraft or specially strengthened their products to enable them to undertake attack missions also. Notable examples include the EMBRAER Super Tucano developed from the successful Tucano trainer for patrol and light attack in the Amazon and the Aermacchi SF.260, variants of which are used for COIN by the Philippines and have a similar role with other air forces. The Pilatus PC-7/9 also performs light attack and the related Raytheon T-6 has a similar capacity while an emerging type is the Korean Aerospace Industries (KAI) KO-1.

Manufacturers of advanced jet trainers have traditionally also offered attack derivatives, sometimes including single-seat machines such as the MB-326K/Impala Mk.2 and the Soko Jastreb while the BAe Hawk 200 and Aero L-159A indeed perform not only attack but fighter roles. The supersonic EADS Mako and KAI T/A-50 are being developed as advanced jet trainers with combat variants. In particular the A-50 is expected to eventually enter service with the Republic of Korea Air Force for CAS. The Alpha Jet A and C-101CC/A-36 light attack machines retain their second seat. Another modern jet trainer that could be used for attack is the Hongdu/Pakistan Aeronautical Complex K-8. The Yakovlev Yak-130 has also been designed to undertake attack duties.

Attack-orientated combat aircraft (that is, as opposed to converted trainers) range from turboprop COIN machines like the Pucara and OV-10. Both have been found to be useful when operated within their design

roles but using these quite limited machines for more ambitious missions could have (and has) been disastrous. Further up the scale are optimised CAS jets like the A-10 and Su-25. The USAF has a love-hate relationship with the A-10 and has preferred to support more glamorous multi-role fighters. However, the aircraft has performed well in recent campaigns and has many years of service ahead of it. Still, it will be replaced by the F-35 Joint Strike Fighter (JSF), one of the new crop of multi-role types. The Russians have praised the performance of the Su-25 in Afghanistan and in Chechnya in the 1980s and 1990s respectively. Unlike the Americans with the A-10, they have continued its development and if the funds are made available the new derivative will enter service. While the A-10 was only bought by the USAF, Russia sold the albeit less radical Su-25 to a number of its allies. Less specialised CAS/tactical attack machines that are more capable in a

The T-50 advanced trainer could be the basis for a future light attack aircraft. Lockheed Martin

wider range of missions though are generally seen as more cost-effective. Examples include the AMX, Jaguar, Orao, A-4, Su-22 and Q-5/A-5. Naval attack machines include the Super Etendard, F-1, F-2 and JH-7. Specialised gunships based on transport aircraft are a rare breed, the ultimate example today being the AC-130 Spectre/Spooky. The AC-130 has proven extremely useful to the US forces in Afghanistan in particular and the US Air Force (USAF) is studying ambitious concepts for its replacement.

The F-35, the most multi-capable combat aircraft ever produced, has been optimised for attack. The European new generation fighters - the Gripen, Rafale and Typhoon - while also very capable in the attack role, are fighters first and are not considered further in this book. Other than in their roles, the F-35 stands apart from these in its dedication to stealth, in the way the systems have been integrated, and in the variety of engine configurations possible. Fast strike fighters which also have multi-role potential include the F-15E,

8 Tornado, Mirage 2000D/N, Su-24, Su-

One concept for the Future Offensive Air System. BAE SYSTEMS

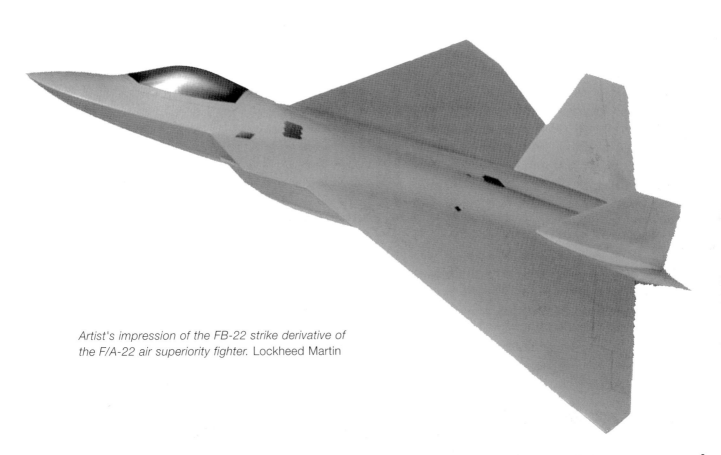

Artist's impression of the FB-22 strike derivative of the F/A-22 air superiority fighter. Lockheed Martin

30MKK and Su-32. The Boeing F/A-18 has been developed to be equally good as fighter and attack aircraft. The Su-32, being evaluated with active stealth technology, holds tremendous promise but lack of finances has delayed its service entry. The USAF's F-15E could well be succeeded by a two-seat FB-22 derivative of the service's F/A-22 air dominance fighter or similar type. For the UK Royal Air Force (RAF), the Future Offensive Air System (FOAS) to replace the Tornado could be met by a combination of manned and unmanned aircraft. Unmanned combat air vehicles (UCAVs) can be effective in attack missions without the possibility of the loss of aircrew. However, costs can quickly grow.

The advent of stealth technology has led to an expansion in the range of attack machines with the F-117A strike aircraft and the B-2 long-range bomber both unique in their respective capabilities. Only the US has the money required to pour into stealth designs and the capabilities of these stealth strike aircraft (and other US stealth types in general) are not likely to be challenged in the foreseeable future. The advent of standoff weaponry has meant that aircraft can operate outside the range of air defences and has given new life to the traditional long-range heavy bomber epitomized by the B-52 and Tu-95. In Operation Enduring Freedom, the USAF's heavy bombers were its most cost-effective aircraft (in terms of cost per weight of tonnage delivered). With the reduction in overseas basing for the US, these aircraft, able to strike from the continental US or from the remaining US bases around the world, are valuable assets.

Recent combat operations have shown the continued (and indeed revitalised) need for CAS aircraft with even heavier aircraft being used. On the other hand, highly accurate long-range cruise missiles increasingly mean that smaller combat aircraft can perform the role previously seen as the forté of the heavy bomber. Poundage though is still a valued characteristic and the B-52 will continue in service for eight decades. More expensive and specialized bombers like the low-level penetration B-1B (or the Tu-160) are harder to justify. Still the US is studying future bomber concepts, with a possible in-service date of 2025-30. One possibility is a hypersonic aircraft. Recent combat experiences will contribute to the determination of future requirements for the US, UK and other air forces. In the 1990s, attack missions at medium altitude became the norm given the threat posed by late-model SAMs. In Operations Enduring Freedom and Iraqi Freedom, air defences did not seriously challenge air power but this is still a relevant concern. In these two campaigns the US's attack types demonstrated rapidly maturing time-critical targeting capabilities, that is, the ability to strike targets a very short time (minutes) after being identified. The US is also improving network-centricity among its air and other forces, with the USAF aiming to eventually transfer information between any sensor and any shooter (attack aircraft) on the battlefield.

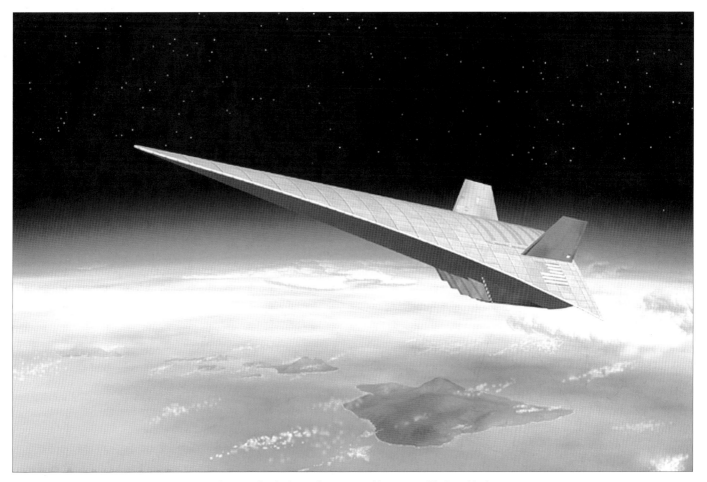

Hypersoar, one concept for a hypersonic attack platform. Lawrence Livermore National Laboratory

Aermacchi MB-326

Aermacchi's MB-326 advanced trainer, which first flew on 10 December 1957, proved to be a tough, manoeuvrable and easily controlled platform and customers (Ghana and Tunisia) ordered armed aircraft early on. Atlas in South Africa assembled or licence-built 111 armed MB-326M models, known as Impala Mk.1, these supplementing forty Italian- produced (unarmed) trainers. The more robust MB-326GB, using the more powerful (15.17 kN) Viper 540 (in place of the Viper 11), doubled the weapons-carrying capacity. Examples were supplied to Argentina, Zaïre (now the DRC) and Zambia. EMBRAER built the similar MB-326GC (as the AT-26 Xavante) for Brazil (167) and others including Paraguay and Togo. Italy and Australia are former MB-326 trainer users.

The aircraft seemed destined to lead to a single-seater combat type and the MB-326K first flew on 22 August 1970. The K, with a stronger airframe, is capable in light attack, reconnaissance and even limited air defence roles. The aircraft could carry a total of 1814 kg of stores on its six underwing hardpoints. These could include free-fall bombs to 454-kg size, 7.62 mm gun pods, rocket launchers, AS11, AS12 or Magic AAMs, or a reconnaissance pod. Gun calibre was increased, a pair of 30 mm DEFA 553 cannon being fitted in the lower fuselage (instead of the trainer's 7.7 mm weapon). Power is provided by the 17.79 kN-thrust Viper 632-43 turbojet.

The DRC, Dubai (the UAE), Ghana and Tunisia received small numbers and some remain in service. Large numbers were licence-produced by Atlas in South Africa as the Impala Mk.2 with different avionics and a lower-thrust Viper 540 turbojet. About thirty-three of these aircraft remain operational in the SAAF where they equip No. 8 Squadron. Cameroon has obtained ex-South African single-and two-seaters. The MB-326L is a two-seat K adopted by the UAE and Tunisia.

Specification: (MB-326K)

First flight: 10 December 1957 (MB-326) and 22 August 1970 (MB-326K)

Current users: Argentina (MB-326GB/EMB-326GB), Brazil (AT/RT-26), Cameroon (Impala Mk.1/Mk.2), DRC (M-326GB/K), Ghana (MB-326K/E), Paraguay (EMB-326), South Africa (Impala Mk.1/Mk.2), Togo (EMB-326G), Tunisia (MB-326B/K/L), UAE (MB-326KD/LD), Zambia (MB-326GB). Includes aircraft used as trainers.

Crew: Two; one (MB-326K/Impala Mk.2).

Wing span: 10.86m

Length: 10.67 m

Height: 3.72 m

Empty weight: 3,123 kg

Max take-off weight: 5,897 kg

Max weapon load: 1,814 kg

Maximum speed: 890 km/h

Maximum range: 268 km combat radius at low altitude; 2,130 km ferry range with two tanks.

Impala Mk.2 of the South African Air Force in flight. World Airnews

Aermacchi MB-339

The MB-339 emerged to fulfil a 1972 Italian air force requirement for a trainer to replace its MB-326s and Aeritalia (then-Fiat) G91Ts. Aermacchi used the MB-326 as the basis and while the MB-339 had a new cockpit with a better view for the instructor and pilot, the fuselage aft of the cockpit was very similar. The first prototype flew on 12 August 1976.

The MB-339 followed its predecessor in employing six underwing weapons stations, maximum payload being 1,815 kg (MB-339C/CD/FD). Weapons could include gun or rocket pods, Magic or Sidewinder AAMs, Martel Mk-2A anti-ship or Maverick anti-surface missile (C/CD/FD) and GP, airfield attack penetration or anti-tank fragmentation bombs. The Italian air force has been evaluating the air-to-air capability of the MB-339 against helicopters and other slow aircraft.

The MB-339A was supplied to Argentina, Dubai (the UAE), Ghana, Italy, Malaysia, Nigeria and Peru, although Argentina has withdrawn its aircraft. Italy also has seventeen similar MB-339PANs, flown by the air force's aerobatic team but which additionally are tasked with light attack. The PAN does not have wingtip fuel tanks. The A was followed by the C with a more powerful 19.57 kN Viper 680-43 turbojet engine and digital avionics; New Zealand received CBs, since acquired by Malaysia, while Eritrea obtained CEs. The most advanced production models are the CD for the home air force and the export equivalent FD (Full Digital), these having a digital nav/attack system, HUD, HOTAS and a 1553B databus. The single-seat MB-339K Veltro 2 attack aircraft with more powerful engine, improved cockpit, greater fuel capacity and fuselage-mounted cannon and the two-seat MB-339AM anti-ship machine with radar did not sell.

Italian aircraft are undergoing a MLU that is seeing their airframes refurbished and a 1553B databus, INS/GPS and other avionics installed.

Specification:
First flight: 12 August 1976 (A)
Current Users: Argentina (A), UAE (A), Eritrea (CE), Ghana (A), Italy (A/CD/ PAN), Malaysia (A/CB), Nigeria (AN) and Peru (AP)
Crew: Two
Wing span: 10 m
Length: 10.972 m
Height: 3.994 m
Empty weight: 3,125 kg
Max take-off weight: 5,900 kg
Max weapon load: 2,040 kg
Maximum speed: 897 km/h
Maximum rate of climb: 2,010 m per minute
Service ceiling: 14,630 m
Maximum range: 1,759 km with full internal fuel

An MB-339PAN sports the colours of the Italian Air Force aerobatic team. Anders Presterud

An AMX at base.
Alenia Aeronautica

Italian Air Force in flight.
Alenia Aeronautica

In 1977, the Italian air force released a requirement for a tactical attack aircraft to replace the F-104G and G91. At the same time Brazil was looking for an attack type to succeed the EMBRAER Xavante. The common requirement led to aircraft companies in the two countries, Aeritalia, Aermacchi and EMBRAER establishing a joint programme to develop a single aircraft.

The resulting AMX was revealed to be simple, reliable and maintainable. It was accurate and efficient and had good endurance and a modern navigation system. The AMX was capable in CAS, interdiction and maritime attack. Italian and Brazilian prototypes first flew on 15 May 1984 and 16 October 1985 respectively. In 1989, production aircraft began joining

the Italian and Brazilian air forces, orders totaling 238 and seventy-nine respectively, including two-seat AMX-T trainers.

The AMX has a single 49.06 kN Rolls Royce Spey RB168-807 turbofan. Italian aircraft use the Grifo X Plus multi-mode pulse Doppler radar while Brazilian models have the SCP-01 Scipio multi-mode coherent radar. Weapons include **17** free-fall, retarded and cluster bombs, rockets, dispensers, precision-guided munitions, air-to-surface, anti-radiation and anti-ship missiles and self-defence air-to-air missiles, to a maximum weight of 3,855 kg. Internal reconnaissance sensors can be supplemented by centreline IR and optical recon pods, laser designator pods (Italy) and IR/EO pods for smart weapons.

The AMI's aircraft are receiving GPS, better early warning capabilities, the CLDP laser designation pod, smart weapons including possibly the JDAM and a real-time reconnaissance pod. Other planned updates are a NVG-compatible cockpit, new HUD, ECM upgrades, Scipio radar, JTIDS MFDs and other avionics modernization. Brazilian aircraft are being fitted with an Elta glass cockpit, new avionics, improved self-defence capabilities and satellite communications capability; further upgrades are to include Scipio radar, HOTAS, night-capable cockpit, improved displays and new datalinks. Venezuela has ordered eight AMX-Ts for advanced training/light attack roles with EL/M-2032 radar and equipment otherwise similar to the modernised Brazilian AMXs.

The AMI's AMXs have had a high accident rate and in particular the aircraft is now thought to be underpowered. Also, it is just as or even more costly than more multi-role contemporary types. Still, Italian aircraft used in Operation Allied Force against Yugoslavia in 1999 achieved an enviable record.

Specification:
First flight: 15 May 1984
Current users: Brazil (AMX/-T) and Italy (AMX/-T). AMX-T ordered by Venezuela
Crew: One (AMX); two (AMX-T)
Wing span: 9.97 m with wingtip missiles
Length: 13.24 m
Height: 4.55 m
Empty weight: 6,700 kg
Max take-off weight: 13,000 kg
Max weapon load: 3,855 kg
Maximum speed: Mach 0.86
Maximum rate of climb: 3,124 m per minute at sea level
Service ceiling: 13,700 m with 50% internal fuel and combat weight of 8,360 kg (for AMX-ATA)
Maximum range: 926 km radius of action; 3,335 km range

Another view of the AMX.
Alenia Aeronautica

Front view of the B-1B. George Canciani

A B-1B with afterburner engaged.
USAF

The B-1A high-altitude penetration nuclear bomber was cancelled in 1977 but developed into the low-altitude stealthier B-1B selected for USAF service. The B-1B, first flew on 18 October 1984. Aircraft began joining the USAF in mid-1985, deliveries continuing to 1988. 100 were received, some of which went to the Air National Guard.

The B-1B uses four 136.71 kN-thrust afterburning General Electric F101-GE-102 turbofans which allow the aircraft to attain an operational speed just below Mach 1. Flight crew consists of a pilot, co-pilot and two weapons systems officers (WSOs), the latter two tasked with the aircraft's offensive and defensive systems respectively.

21

The aircraft has been plagued with maintenance problems and a low mission-capable rate throughout its career. Cracks in the structure have also been a problem. Another source of concern was the ALQ-161A electronic self-defence system. In the early 1990s, plans were being made to improve this system but operational analysis indicated that the resulting aircraft still would not be able to penetrate Soviet air defence and the aircraft was relieved of the strategic nuclear bombing role. The fleet has been receiving GPS and communications modifications among other improvements and further under the Block E upgrade the aircraft are being fitted with a new computer and the WCMD. Still, some of the B-1Bs are now being retired. Funds saved were to have been used to undertake a Defensive Systems Upgrade Programme (DSUP) of the remaining aircrafts' ALQ-161A but this was cancelled. Existing systems are now to receive a more limited upgrade. The JASSM, JSOW and WCMD standoff weapons are being integrated, with consideration being given to changing the role of the aircraft to standoff weapons launch.

Despite its poor maintenance record, the B-1B *did* perform well in strike missions against Iraq in December 1988. Also, B-1Bs performed night bombing missions over Afghanistan in Operation Enduring Freedom (2001-2002) in which they were responsible for 39 % of the weapons dropped, a higher proportion than any other aircraft type and at a mission-capable rate approaching 90 %. However, the Afghan integrated air defence system (IADS) encountered was not sophisticated. The B-1B was also used in Operation Iraqi Freedom in March-April 2003 where JDAM-armed aircraft provided round-the-clock presence over the country. This enabled the B-1Bs to rapidly respond to time-critical targets.

Specification:
First flight: 18 October 1984
Current users: US
Crew: Four
Wing span: 41.67m spread; 23.84 m swept
Length: 44.81 m
Height: 10.24 m
Empty weight: 86,260 kg
Max take-off weight: 216,558 kg
Max weapon load: 34,019 kg
Maximum speed: Mach 1.25
Service ceiling: Over 9,144 km
Maximum range: 12,000 km

A USAF B-1B delivers its load of weapons. USAF

23

B-52H of the USAF.
Keith Blincow

First flying as a prototype on 15 April 1952, the B-52 has been the mainstay of the US airborne nuclear deterrent for most of its service life, a role that it now shares with the B-2. The B-52s now concentrate much more on conventional bombing although they can quickly change weapons carriage between conventional and nuclear. At the end of the Cold War, two subtypes were in service, the conventional-tasked B-52G and the nuclear B-52H.

Another view of the B-52.
USAF

The B-52Gs were more versatile but older and fell victim to the post-Cold War force draw-downs. The B-52Hs, the last production version, had more structural life and more powerful and maintainable turbofans. The ninety-four B-52Hs remained in service but only eighty of these have the Common Strategic Rotary Launcher (CSRL). Further, under the SALT II arms reduction treaty, only sixty-six of the ALCM-capable aircraft are allowed and the remaining twenty-eight are officially spares; one aircraft has gone to NASA. The B-52H fleet is based at two locations in the US.

The CSRL could dispense the AGM-86 ALCM, or B-53, B-61 or B-83 nuclear bombs. With the retirement of the B-52Gs, the B-52Hs were given the capability to launch the AGM-142 Have Nap and AGM-84 Harpoon ASMs. The aircraft also received a MIL-STD-1760 weapons databus. The Advanced Weapons Integration programme is resulting in the B-52s being modified to use the WCMD, JDAM, JSOW and JASSM while future options include the Extended Range CM and SDB. The B-61 is also being improved.

GPS has been installed. The aircraft's FLIR is being replaced and ECM capability being upgraded. The cockpit has also been made more NVG-compatible. One of the most significant upgrades to the aircraft though is the Avionics Midlife Improvement (AMI) in which INS and data links among other components are being upgraded. The Litening-2 laser target-designating pod made its combat debut in Operation Iraqi Freedom. The B-52 could also be given an electronic attack responsibility. The aircraft is currently powered by eight 76 kN-thrust Pratt & Whitney TF33-P-3 turbofans. However, spurred on by recent operations which demonstrated the need for fuel efficiency and low cost, the USAF is studying the installation of new engines.

The B-52 is expected to remain in service to at least 2040, by which time the aircraft will have been in the USAF for eighty-five years.

Specification:
First flight: 15 April 1952
Current users: US
Crew: Six
Wing span: 56.39 m
Length: 49.05 m
Height: 12.4 m
Empty weight: 83,990 kg
Max take-off weight: 221,552 kg
Max weapon load: 31,780 kg
Maximum speed: Mach 0.9
Service ceiling: 16,764 m
Maximum range: Over 16,900 km.

A B-52 releases its bombload.
USAF

*A USAF air-to-air armed F-15E
being refuelled.* USAF

An armed F-15I sporting air-to-ground camouflage. Keith Blincow

The F-15E is a long-range strike fighter derivative of the F-15 air superiority fighter. The aircraft, whose airframe is strengthened compared to previous models for greater operational weights, can conduct attack missions without fighter escort. The first production F-15E made its maiden flight on 11 December 1986.

The F-15E uses the AN/APG-70 radar which has a synthetic aperture mode for ground attack and which is also capable in the air-to-air role. The aircraft is powered by a pair of Pratt & Whitney F100-PW-220 or F100-PW-229 turbofans each producing 105.74 kN or 129.445 kN with reheat respectively. The reliability

Another USAF F-15E.
Sven deBevere

and maintainability of these engines have contributed to the Strike Eagle's unequalled safety record. Conformal fuel tanks hold 5,508 litres of fuel but additionally drop tanks can be carried.

The F-15E has eighteen hardpoints for weapons and stores but this number can be increased by the use of multiple ejectors. Total payload is theoretically 11,113 kg, but 10,432 kg in practice. The air-to-surface arsenal includes Maverick, HARM and AGM-130 missiles, free-fall and guided bombs including JDAM and nuclear bombs. A future weapon is the WCMD. F-15Es retain a substantial air-to-air capability and weapons include Sidewinder, Sparrow and AMRAAM. Other possible stores include LANTIRN navigation and target designation pods and the high-speed anti-radar missile targeting system (HTS). Some USAF F-15Es will receive Litening ER targeting pods to replace older LANTIRN systems. The starboard wing contains a 20 mm Vulcan M61A1 six-barrel cannon.

Deliveries to the USAF began in 1988, the total ordered by the service being 236. Saudi Arabia received the last of its F-15Ss in 2000. Forty-eight of the Saudi aircraft are for attack, the remaining twenty-four for fighter duties. The F-15Ss are downgraded compared to USAF F-15Es, and do not have terrain mapping (using a degraded APG-70), LANTIRN and as sophisticated an EW capability. Israel received its twenty-five F-15I Ra'am (Thunder) aircraft between 1998 and 1999. Israeli aircraft have some indigenous systems including a display and sight helmet system (DASH) and different EW/self-defence suites. They can also use the local Python 4 AAM.

On 19 April 2002, South Korea selected the F-15K, a version of the F-15E, for its F-X strike fighter requirement. Forty aircraft will be acquired with options on a further forty. The F-15K will use the General Electric F110-129 engine. They will have a modern datalink, improved electronic self-defence systems, helmet-mounted cueing system, new FLIR and APG-63 radar. Armament will include JDAM, JSOW, Harpoon and AGM-130 or AGM-142 as well as HARM air-to-surface weapons and AAMs. South Korea also wants the JASSM for a standoff capability but the US is only allowing the SLAM-ER missile. The F-15K will be the most advanced F-15E derivative.

Specification:
First flight: 11 December 1996
Current users: Israel (F-15I), Saudi Arabia (F-15S) and US (F-15E); intended for South Korea (F-15K)
Crew: Two
Wing span: 13.05 m
Length: 19.45 m
Height: 5.63 m
Empty weight: 14,515 kg
Max take-off weight: 36,740 kg
Max weapon load: 11,113 kg
Maximum speed: Mach 2.5
Service ceiling: 18,290 m
Maximum range: 1,217 km combat radius; 4,445 km range with full fuel.

An armed RAF Harrier II in flight. The type's large engine inlets are apparent. RAF/Crown Copyright

The much-improved development of the revolutionary first-generation V/STOL Harrier CAS/interdiction aircraft first flew on 5 November 1981. The new aircraft retained the same basic configuration of its predecessor, the Harrier family still unique among today's combat aircraft in using a four-poster vectored-thrust turbofan to enable STOVL performance and with control continuing to be provided by not only ailerons and flaps (and slab tailplane and rudder) but also by wingtip, nose and tail reaction controls that use engine bleed air. The Harrier II introduced new high-lift devices, bigger wings and LERXs (leading edge root extensions), composites, upgraded engine, and new avionics which allow it to boast twice the payload/range capability of the earlier aircraft. The aircraft uses a single Rolls Royce Pegasus 11 high-bypass-ratio turbofan, the latest, most capable and versatile Mk 107 (Pegasus 11-61) providing 105.87 kN of thrust.

Another view of the Harrier.
RAF/Crown Copyright

GR.Mk7s, the current RAF standard, have nine hardpoints and USMC AV-8Bs seven. Pegasus 11-61-powered aircraft can lift 6,000 kg. Payload can include free-fall, laser-guided (including Paveway series) and cluster bombs, rocket launchers, Maverick and other ASMs and Sidewinder/Magic AAMs. JSOW will be integrated on USMC aircraft while the RAF versions will be fitted with Brimstone, Storm Shadow and ASRAAM.

The AV-8B entered USMC service in early 1984. From the 167th production aircraft, USMC Harrier IIs were of the Night Attack standard with FLIR, and the Pegasus 11-61 engine. These aircraft have an angle rate bombing system (ARBS).

The RAF began receiving its ninety-six second-generation aircraft from mid-1987. These have been converted to the night attack GR.Mk7, not dissimilar to the USMC update. Thirteen T.Mk10 trainers are of a corresponding standard. GR.Mk7As have the Mk 107 powerplant. Harriers emerging from the Integrated Weapons Programme (IWP) are to be redesignated GR.Mk9/9A depending on the engine installed (Mk105 or 107), the first aircraft modernised to GR.9 standard flying on 30 May 2003. T.Mk10s will become T.Mk12s. The RAF's upgraded Harriers will have a Mil Std 1760 weapons databus, a new computer, improved sensors, new displays, GPS/INS and secure communications and new IFF system. The service's aircraft have a TIALD capability and other reconnaissance assets may also be carried.

The Harrier II Plus first flew on 22 September 1992. This aircraft has an APG-65 multi-mode radar and can undertake all-weather, day/night attack and BVR air-to-air operations. New or re-built aircraft began entering service with the USMC in 1993 and with the Italian and Spanish navies. RAF Harrier IIs used the Maverick missile and Enhanced Paveway PGB in combat for the first time during Operation Iraqi Freedom in early 2003 while USMC Harrier II Pluses demonstrated a real-time strike capability with the Litening II pod. Notably in this operation Harriers were the only aircraft that could be forward deployed close to advancing ground forces.

Specification:
First flight: 5 November 1981
Current users: Italy (AV-8B+/TAV-8B), Spain (EAV-8B/B+), UK (Harrier GR7/9/T10/12) and US (AV-8B/B+/TAV-8B)
Crew: Pilot; two for trainer versions.
Wing span: 9.25 m
Length: 14.53 m (GR.7) and 14.12 m (AV-8B)
Height: 3.56 m
Empty weight: 6,831 kg (GR7) and 6,337 kg (AV-8B)
Max take-off weight: 14,061-14,515 kg for STO
Max weapon load: 6,000 kg for Pegasus 11-61-powered aircraft
Maximum speed: Mach 0.91-0.98
Maximum range: 1,111 km radius of action with two 454 kg bombs, two cluster bombs and two drop tanks. Over 2,963/3,334 km ferry range for GR7/AV-8B.

RAF Harriers operate from a Royal Navy vessel. RAF/Crown Copyright

Cessna A-37B Dragonfly   USA

The USAF Special Air Warfare Centre in the early 1960s began examining the possible use of a re-engined T-37 trainer in the COIN role. The new engine, the General Electric J85-GE-5 turbojet offered 10.68 kN of thrust, more than twice that of the T-37's original powerplant. The just-beginning Vietnam conflict seemed to confirm the need for such an aircraft and 39 retired T-37Bs were so-converted, being re-designated A-37 Dragonfly. The cockpit was armoured and the nose had a GAU-2B/A 7.62 mm Gatling gun. The aircraft's 8 under-wing hardpoints could carry GP, incendiary or cluster bombs, rocket pods, and gun pods, maximum payload being 1,360 kg. Wingtip tanks were also installed. A-37s were supplied to the USAF from May 1967 and many were evaluated in Vietnam and went on to serve with the South Vietnam air force. The type was found to be more accurate than faster combat aircraft. Another variant is the A-37B. It had a stronger airframe, greater internal fuel capacity and the ability to carry more fuel externally and could be refuelled in flight. It introduced self-sealing fuel tanks and improved navigation systems. The A-37B first flew in September 1967 and deliveries began the following year. 577 were produced, the last in 1977. The A-37B was later also re-designated OA-37B for FAC (with radios added).

A-37s went not only to the USAF and to South Vietnam but also to the US Air National Guard and air forces in Latin America, Thailand and South Korea. Some Ecuadorian aircraft were modified to use Israeli Shafir II AAMs.

Specification:
First flight: 22 October 1963 (A-37A) and September 1967 (A-37B)
Current users: Chile, Colombia, Dominican Republic, Ecuador, El Salvador, Guatemala, Honduras, Paraguay, Peru, South Korea and Uruguay
Crew: Two
Wing span: 10.93 m with wingtip tanks
Length: 8.62 m without probe
Height: 2.8 m
Empty weight: 2,817 kg
Max take-off weight: 6,350 kg
Max weapon load: 1,360 kg
Maximum speed: 816 km/h
Maximum rate of climb: 2,130 m per minute initial
Service ceiling: 12,730 m
Maximum range: 740 km range at high altitude with maximum payload.

An A-37B of the Chilean Air Force.
Chilean Air Force

A French Air Force Mirage 2000N, the weapon
load including underfuselage ASMP and
underwing Magic missiles. Dassault Aviation

The Mirage 2000N was conceived as a high-speed low-level nuclear strike aircraft to succeed the Mirage IIIE and Jaguar A, Dassault once again turning to the tailless configuration that had proved so successful in the Mirage 2000 and earlier Mirage series. First flight of a prototype Mirage 2000N occurred on 3 February 1983 with a production example following in March 1986. The first of 75 aircraft began entering AdA service in 1988.

An armed French Air Force Mirage 2000D in flight. Dassault Aviation

Power is provided by a SNECMA M53-P2 turbofan producing 95.19 kN with reheat. Avionics include the Antilope 5 TFR, representing the first such capability in the AdA. Primary armament is the ASMP medium-range nuclear ASM, the first Mirage 2000Ns being restricted to this weapon and Magic self-defence AAMs. Later aircraft have improved conventional capability however, being able to use free fall, anti-runway and area-denial (cluster) bombs although not precision conventional weapons.

Low-level operations include flight at less than 100m but speed is mostly subsonic. The second crewman performs navigation, and self-defence duties. Despite a Mirage 2000N being lost to a SAM over Bosnia in mid-1995, ECM capability has impressed in NATO exercises and additionally has been further improved by updates, in particular the installation of a missile launch detector (DDM). ASMP will be succeeded by the more accurate and longer-ranged ASMP-A while the Reco NG pod will enable reconnaissance to be undertaken.

40   The Mirage 2000D emerged as a conventional precision strike version of the 2000N. The programme was launched in 1988 and first flight occurred on 19 February 1991. The first aircraft entered the AdA in July 1993, achieving FOC the next year. Deliveries continued to 2001 with the total order being for eighty-six aircraft.

The cockpit has significant improvements, including the Antilope 5-3D radar and other new avionics and systems. Anti-radiation and anti-ship missiles, laser-guided weapons, free-fall, anti-runway and cluster bombs and 30 mm gun and rocket pods are weapon options but ASMP cannot be used. Later aircraft can carry the Apache dispenser, Atlis II or PDL-CT/S laser designator pod and a more advanced self-protection system. The second crewman is responsible for laser designation, having more duties than his Mirage 2000N counterpart. Some of the earlier Mirage 2000Ds were upgraded to the newer standard. The Scalp EG stealth CM is being integrated on the aircraft while a future weapon package is the AASM guidance kit. French Mirage 2000Ds performed attack missions in Operations Allied Force and Enduring Freedom in 1999 and 2002 respectively.

Specification:
First flight: 3 February 1983
Current users: France
Crew: Two
Wing span: 9.13 m
Length: 14.65 m
Height: 5.15 m
Empty weight: 8,175 kg
Max take-off weight: 17,500 kg
Max weapon load: 6,300 kg
Maximum speed: Over Mach 2.2
Maximum rate of climb: 18,300 m per minute
Service ceiling: 18,300 m
Maximum range: 1,445 km range with five minutes combat at medium altitude and carrying six AAMs; over 3,520 km range with drop tanks

Another French Mirage 2000D.
Rafael Finter

Dassault Super Etendard   France

The Etendard (Flag), the predecessor of today's Super Etendard, emerged in response to a 1953 NATO requirement for a light strike fighter. The aircraft was not chosen but variants of it went on to see service with the French Navy in attack and reconnaissance roles. However, by the late 1960s the service was looking for a replacement type.

A navalized Anglo-French Jaguar and US aircraft were considered but a development of the Etendard was eventually selected. Compared to the Etendard the new aircraft had a new engine, the 50.107 kN-thrust Snecma Atar 8K 50 turbojet, new wing and modern weapons system. The Super Etendard made its maiden flight on 28 October 1974. The aircraft entered service in 1978, production continuing to 1983 during which time eighty-five aircraft were built. The Super Etendard has an Agave air-to-air and air-to-surface-capable radar and, when armed with the AM39 Exocet anti-ship missile, represents a very powerful asset, as the UK found to its cost in the 1982 Falklands War.

The Argentine Navy obtained twelve aircraft, with the French Navy having fifty-four modernised examples, the first upgraded aircraft flying on 5 October 1990. The aircraft was updated to fire the ASMP ASM. Continuing phased upgrades have led to the ultimate Super Etendard Modernised (SEM) standard. The SEM has an updated cockpit with new displays, the more powerful and versatile Anemone radar, ATLIS laser designation pod usable with the AS30L ASM and LGBs, updated self-defence capability and Magic II IR-guided AAMs. The aircraft retains two internal 30mm DEFA 552 guns but when the above ASMs are carried they cannot be used. The CRM280 recon pod allows the SEM to replace the previously specialist Etendard IV photo-recce aircraft. Under the latest phase of the SEM update, the aircraft is being given a night attack capability, based on the Damocles laser-designation pod, and navigation systems are being improved. The Super Etendard will provide an airborne attack capability for the French Navy to at least 2011.

Specification:
First flight: 28 October 1974
Current users: France and Argentina
Crew: Pilot
Wing span: 9.6 m
Length: 14.31 m
Height: 3.85 m
Empty weight: 6,450 kg
Max take-off weight: 11,500 kg
Max weapon load: 2,500 kg
Maximum speed: Mach 1
Maximum rate of climb: 7,500 m per minute initial
Service ceiling: 13,700 m
Maximum range: 650 km radius with one AM39 and one tank

A French Navy Super Etendard.
Colin Norwood

The Alpha Jet was selected in 1970 to meet a Franco-German joint trainer requirement of the previous year. Germany later also specified light attack and reconnaissance capabilities and two slightly different variants emerged, the attack-orientated Alpha Jet A and the trainer Alpha Jet E for Germany and France respectively.

Both versions were constructed primarily of metal and with a high-mounted wing and were powered by a pair of 13.24 kN-thrust SNECMA/Turbomeca Larzac 04-C6 turbojets. The Alpha Jet prototype made its maiden flight on 26 October 1973, the A following on 9 January 1974. This version had a maximum payload of 2,500 kg carried on a hardpoint under the fuselage centre and four under the wings and which could include rockets, free-fall and cluster bombs, Maverick ASMs, fuel tanks, and recce and ECM pods. A 27 mm Mauser cannon was also fitted. Avionics included a simple navigation and weapon-aiming system with a

An Alpha Jet A of the Portuguese Air Force. Sven De Bevere

HUD. Agile, flyable and maintainable, the Alpha Jet soon proved itself to be a cost-effective attack machine.

German aircraft formed three attack wings and a training squadron. Portugal received fifty ex-German aircraft. Germany has since retired its Alphas, some being sold to Thailand (twenty) and the UK (twelve) with others still on offer. The Alternative CAS version with inertial navigation, HUD, laser ranger and radar altimeter was assembled in Egypt as the MS2, fifteen joining thirty earlier attack-optimised MS1s in the Egyptian air force. Cameroon also received MS2s.

A further evolution was the Alpha Jet 2 (previously known as the NGEA) with MS2 systems, the higher-power Larzac 04-C20 engine and a greater payload including Magic AAMs. The ultimate Alpha was the Lancier with an Agave radar and glass cockpit among other avionics and systems improvements and an expanded weapons range. Both these developments however failed to attract buyers.

France received large numbers of the Alpha Jet E, this variant using the 30mm DEFA cannon in place of the

German gun. Other E model recipients are Belgium, Ivory Coast, Morocco, Nigeria, Qatar and Togo. Belgian Alpha Jets are being upgraded. French aircraft may also be modernised.

Specification:
First flight: 26 October 1973 (Alpha Jet); 9 January 1974 (A)
Current users: Belgium (E), Cameroon (MS2), Egypt (MS1/2), France (E), Ivory Coast (E), Morocco (E), Nigeria (E), Portugal (A), Qatar (E), Togo (E/MS1), Thailand (A) and the UK (A). Includes aircraft used as trainers
Crew: Two
Wing span: 9.11 m
Length: 12.29 m without probe
Height: 4.19 m
Empty weight: 3,345 kg
Max take-off weight: 7,500 kg
Max weapon load: 2,500 kg
Maximum speed: Mach 0.85
Maximum rate of climb: 3,420 m per minute at sea level
Service ceiling: 14,630 m
Maximum range: 425 km radius at low altitude with four 227 kg bombs

The C-101 was developed by CASA to replace the Spanish air force's HA-200/220 trainer/attack aircraft. US and German companies helped in the development of the new aircraft and substantial US components were used. First flight occurred on 27 June 1977. The C-101EB entered Spanish service as the E.25.

The C-101 was chosen as the basis for a 1978 Chilean requirement for a successor to the country's A-37 Dragonfly and T-37 Tweety aircraft in the CAS and advanced training roles respectively. It was considered advanced, had a widely available civilian engine and could be assembled locally, developed further and was affordable. Operationally it had long range, a tough airframe, wide weapons range and good aircrew visibility. The power-to-weight ratio though was thought to be low.

In the first instance, fourteen examples of a re-engined version, the C-101BB entered Chilean service (as the T-36) to fulfil the trainer

Chilean Air Force A-36.
Chilean Air Force

requirement, although the aircraft also had an attack capability. Chilean C-101s are known as Halcon (Falcon).

CASA and ENAER together developed an attack-optimised version in which engine power is further boosted, the C-101CC, designated the A-36 by the Chileans. The C-101CC uses the Garett AiResearch TFE731-5-1J turbofan which provides 19.12 kN of thrust. A fuselage bay could accommodate a 30 mm DEFA 553 (used in Chilean aircraft) or two Browning 12.7mm guns or reconnaissance, laser-designation or ECM pods. A further 2,250 kg of weapons, including rocket pods, bombs and Sidewinder, Magic and Maverick missiles can be deployed on six underwing hardpoints. Twenty-three A-36s were obtained to equip two combat groups of the Chilean air force. Jordan also bought C-101CCs.

A Chilean development was the A-36M with upgraded avionics and the ability to launch the Sea Eagle anti-ship missile (despite the aircraft not having radar) but this project was cancelled. The SAGEM Maestro nav/attack system, already in Chilean

service with the modernised Mirage 5M Elkan, formed the basis of an A-36 upgrade, the new aircraft being designated Halcon II. The update includes INS/GPS, HUD, HOTAS and MFDs. The upgraded aircraft can use the Shafrir II AAM.

Specification: (C-101CC)
First flight: 27 June 1977 (C-101), 16 November 1983 (C-101CC).
Current users: Chile (A/T-36), Honduras (C-101BB), Jordan (C-101CC) and Spain (E25). Includes aircraft used as trainers
Crew: Two
Wing span: 10.60 m
Length: 12.50 m
Height: 4.25 m
Max take-off weight: 6,300 kg
Max weapon load: 2,250 kg
Maximum speed: 834 km/h
Maximum rate of climb: 1,494 m per minute at sea level
Service ceiling: 12,800 m
Maximum range: 602 km radius with two Mavericks, DEFA cannon pack and fuel reserve

EMBRAER EMB-312/314 Tucano/Super Tucano   Brazil

A US embargo on defence equipment to Brazil in the mid-1970s compelled that nation to develop its own combat aircraft, the result being the EMBRAER EMB-312 Tucano (Toucan, also designated T-27) combat-capable basic trainer. The Tucano first flew on 16 August 1980 under the power of a 559.3 kW Pratt & Whitney Canada PT6A-25C turboprop engine. Four underwing hardpoints could accommodate 1,000 kg of weapons including gun pods, rocket launchers and bombs. Argentina, Egypt, France, Iran, Iraq, Kuwait, Peru, the UK and Venezuela received aircraft for training, AOI in Egypt and Short Brothers in the UK building the type under licence. Angola, Brazil, Colombia, Honduras, Kenya and Paraguay specified armed aircraft for training and COIN/light attack.

An armed Super Tucano EMBRAER

EMBRAER continued evolving the design, flying the EMB-314 Super Tucano in May 1993 and that year also saw work beginning on a further developed version, the EMB-314M ALX, to undertake day/night border patrol and intruder missions in addition to advanced training. On 18 August 1995 the company received a contract from the Brazilian Air Force for the development of the ALX in single- (designated A-29 by the service) and two-seat (AT-29) versions. The first so-converted Super Tucano flew in May 1996. The comprehensive range of systems is comparable to that of modern frontline combat types, avionics being supplied by Elbit. The pilot is protected by Kevlar armour and the aircraft has been designed to use rough airstrips. Power is provided by the 1,193 kW Pratt & Whitney Canada PT6A-68/3. The ALX has a pair of 12.7 mm guns in the wings. Five pylons can accommodate a 1,500 kg payload that could include the Maverick missile, free-fall bombs, unguided rockets and a 20 mm gun pod. Self-defence AAMs are an option. The AT-29 can use a FLIR for night missions.

The aircraft can attain 454 km/h when carrying a representative payload. The A-29 has an extra 300 litres of fuel compared to the AT-29 which gives it an endurance of seven hours. Cost is $4.5-5 million depending on equipment fit.

The Brazilian Air Force is obtaining 99 ALXs including 44 A-29s and 20 AT-29s for day and night patrol of the Amazon respectively (and 30 aircraft for training), the first aircraft having being received in December 2003. The Dominican Republic has ordered 12 Super Tucanos.

Specification: (EMB-314)

First flight: 16 August 1980, 15 May 1993 and May 1996 for EMB-312, EMB-314, and ALX conversion of EMB-314 respectively

Current users: Angola (EMB-312), Argentina (EMB-312), Brazil (EMB-312/314), Colombia (EMB-312), Egypt (EMB-312), France (EMB-312), Honduras (EMB-312), Iran (EMB-312), Iraq (EMB-312), Kenya (EMB-312), Kuwait (EMB-312), Paraguay (EMB-312), Peru (EMB-312), the UK (T1) and Venezuela (EMB-312). Includes aircraft used as trainers. EMB-314 on order for the Dominican Republic

Crew: Pilot; two for trainer versions.

Wing span: 11.14 m

Length: 11.42 m

Height: 3.9 m

Empty weight: 2,420 kg

Max take-off weight: 3,190 kg

Max weapon load: 1,500 kg

Maximum speed: over 556 km/h at 6,100 m

Maximum rate of climb: 895 m per minute

Service ceiling: 10,650 m

Maximum range: 1,853 km, fully armed **49**

General Dynamics F-111

US

The F-111 long-range, all-weather VG strike aircraft made its maiden flight on 21 December 1964. F-111s were delivered to the USAF, these being retired by mid-1997, and to the current operator, the RAAF.

The USAF used striker/bomber F-111As, D, E, F (with TAC) and FB-111s (SAC) and EW EF-111As as well as the trainer F-111G (converted from the FB-111). Australia selected the F-111C in late 1963 for long-range strike and

reconnaissance but the twenty-four aircraft only arrived in the country a decade later. The RF-111C was also obtained. The first batch has been supplemented by four former USAF F-111As to replace attrition losses, these

An F-111 of the RAAF.
Alastair McBean

50

aircraft being converted to F-111Cs. Additionally fifteen ex-USAF F-111Gs were acquired from 1993 (and further reserve airframes and extra engines since obtained). Two squadrons operate the RAAF's thirty-five aircraft of the three marks. This force was operationally used for the first time in late 1999 when F-111s flew reconnaissance missions over East Timor as part of an Australian-led UN peace operation.

The aircraft can carry 14,288 kg of weapons and stores, F-111Cs being powered by two 82.29 kN-thrust Pratt & Whitney TF30-P-3 afterburning turbofans. In the mid-1980s, Australian aircraft received the Pave Tack day/night laser designator pod and the Harpoon anti-ship missile. The analogue cockpits were also modernised to a digital standard enabling the range of weapons to be expanded (although the cannon was removed). RF-111s received a more modest upgrade. The RAAF, though, has been trying to improve fleet commonality. More recently the F-111s have received modernised electronic self-defence systems and the service is also integrating the AGM-142E standoff weapon. The RAAF has also been conducting F-111 flight evaluations of an active separation control (ASC) system to enhance weapons bay acoustics and assist weapons release, representative small smart bombs (SSBs) having been used in the tests. Wing structure problems are a concern though. In late 2003 the planned retirement date was brought forward by 5-10 years to 2010.

Specification: (F-111C)
First flight: 21 December 1964 (F-111A)
Current users: Australia
Crew: Two
Wing span: 21.34 m spread; 10.34 m swept
Length: 22.40 m
Height: 5.22 m
Empty weight: 21,455 kg
Max take-off weight: 45,360 kg
Max weapon load: 14,288 kg
Maximum speed: Mach 2.2
Maximum range: 5,093 km with maximum internal fuel.

Harbin H-5 (B-5) & Ilyushin IL-28 "Beagle"   China/Russia

The Ilyushin Il-28, NATO codename "Beagle", is a first-generation medium/high-altitude bomber which first flew in August 1948 and which became the first jet bomber in the Soviet Union. The Il-28 is powered by a development of the British-supplied Rolls Royce Nene turbojet, the 26.87 kN-thrust VK-1 Klimov and is also notable for its wing configuration, the main wing having a straight leading and swept trailing edge while the tail wing is swept.

The Il-28 also entered service with Soviet client states and was produced in China and Czechoslovakia. Russo-Chinese relations were good when the Il-28 aircraft deals were first struck but suffered later, and China was forced to reverse-engineer areas of the structure and to develop some new systems. A Chinese Harbin-built aircraft first flew as the H-5 on 25 September 1966. The H-5's Wopen WP-5A engine was a derivative of the Il-28's Klimov VK-1A while standard armament included a twin 23 mm cannon-equipped tail turret and a weapons bay for bombs and torpedoes.

Harbin developed the H-5A version to carry nuclear weapons. Another Chinese variant is the HJ-5 (BT-5) bomber trainer (NATO codename "Mascot") which has a second cockpit in the fuselage ahead of the main raised cockpit and the ventral fairing and glazed nose removed. The HZ-5 (BR-5) reconnaissance aircraft has a camera-equipped bomb bay and wing-mounted fuel tanks while the HD-5 is an EW variant. A PLAN version has Yu-2 torpedoes. Chinese production lasted sixteen years with the last aircraft built in the 1980s and during which time the PLAAF and PLAN received 500 and 130 machines respectively. In the late 1980s though, China began withdrawing H-5s from service. China also exported aircraft to North Korea and Romania. North Korea, which still has the type on strength, obtained aircraft from China and also from the Soviet Union. Romania also received H-5s from China including the reconnaissance H-5R but only a few flyable examples remain.

Specification:
First flight: August 1948 (Il-28); 25 September 1966 (H-5)
Current users: China, North Korea and Romania
Crew: Three
Wing span: 21.45 m
Length: 16.77 m
Height: 6.2 m
Max take-off weight: 21,200 kg
Max weapon load: 3,000 kg
Maximum speed: 902 km/h at 4,500 m
Maximum rate of climb: 900 m per minute at sea level
Service ceiling: 12,300 m
Maximum range: 2,400 km at 10,000 m

Two of Romania's remaining H-5s. Hugo Mambour/AviaScribe

Hongdu Q-5/A-5 "Fantan" China

An A-5C of the Pakistan Air Force.
Abbas Ali

The Q-5 (A-5), NATO codename "Fantan", supersonic attack aircraft is China's first indigenous combat aircraft, though derived largely from the Soviet MiG-19 and its Chinese version, the Shenyang J-6. The most marked external change from these types is the installation of a solid nose (without radar) and a pair of fuselage-side-mounted engine inlets instead of the nose inlet, the new configuration allowing the fitting of an internal weapons bay. Close air support is an important role and the Q-5 also boasts armour protection for the pilot.

Design of the Q-5 began in 1958 but the programme was cancelled in 1961 only to be restarted two years later. The prototype first flew on 5 June 1965 but substantial redesign was required before production aircraft could be fielded from 1970.

The early Q-5 suffered from short range but this was rectified in the Q-5 I first seen in 1980 and which went on to become the most prolific model. The greater internal fuel of the Q-5 I, however, came at the cost of the bomb bay and also in turn meant that a further two underwing pylons had to

be fitted. PLAN Q-5 Is could carry torpedoes and C-801 anti-ship missiles. The Q-5 IA with six underwing stations appeared in 1984 and was exported to North Korea. The similar Q-5 II has improved avionics and can carry laser-guided weapons.

In 1983, the Pakistan air force began receiving its specially developed variant the A-5C (or A-5 III) developed from the Q-5 I and able to carry Western weapons. Bangladesh and Myanmar also received A-5Cs.

From the mid-1980s, collaboration with French and Italian companies was begun and lead to two new versions, the Q-5K and Q-5M, but both programmes were aborted, although A-5Ms were supplied to Myanmar in 1993. A day/night, all-weather-capable Q-5D model has also been identified while in the late 1990s manufacture of the Q-5E/F was begun. The Q-5A designation refers to a handful of nuclear-capable aircraft.

Q-5s are powered by a pair of Liming WP6 turbojets while A-5s use two WP6As. With afterburning these are capable of 31.87 kN and 39.72 kN thrust respectively.

Specification: (for A-5C where relevant)
First flight: 5 June 1965 (Q-5)
Current users: China (Q-5), Bangladesh (A-5C), Pakistan (A-5C), Myanmar (A-5C/M) and North Korea (A-5)
Crew: Pilot
Wing span: 9.7 m
Length: 16.77 m with probe
Height: 4.52 m
Empty weight: 6,638 kg
Max take-off weight: 12,200 kg
Max weapon load: 2,000 kg
Maximum speed: 1,210 km/h (at sea level)
Maximum rate of climb: 8,880 m per minute at sea level
Service ceiling: 15,850 m
Maximum range: 400-600 km radius with 2,000 kg payload; 1,816 km range with full fuel at 11,000 m and optimum speed

Head-on view of an AC-130.
USAF

The AC-130H and AC-130U are respectively second and third generation USAF C-130-derived gunships. The AC-130H became operational with the USAF in 1972 while the AC-130U, which first flew on 20 December 1990, became operational in 1995. The gunships perform CAS, air interdiction, reconnaissance and related missions.

The aircraft are powered by four 3362 kW Allison T56-A-15 turboprops. Armament for the AC-130H consists of a pair of M61 20 mm Vulcan cannons with 4,000 rounds, an L60 40 mm Bofors cannon (256 rounds) and an M102 105 mm howitzer (100). The AC-130U has similar weapons except that a 25 mm Gatling gun, capable of 1,800 rounds per minute, replaces the Vulcans. Aircrew number 14 and 13 for the AC-130H and AC-130U respectively. The USAF's 8/13 AC-130H/Us are operated by the 16th Special Operations Wing at Hurlburt Field in Florida.

AC-130 aircraft pioneered manned aircraft-UAV coordination in Operation Enduring Freedom of 2001/2 where Predator UAVs conducted reconnaissance and transmitted data directly to the gunships enabling the latter to strike time-critical targets in a matter of minutes. The conflict has spurred gunship renewal programmes. Eight further AC-130Us are being obtained and additionally AC-130Hs are being converted to AC-130Us. The wings are being strengthened and under-wing fuel tanks replaced with wingtip models. The current All-Light-Level TV (ALLTV) is planned to be replaced by a system that is capable in more spectrums and has a 360° field of view. The AC-130s will also undergo an Avionics Modernization Programme (AMP). Further new EO and IR sensors and computers are to be installed. The 30 mm GAU-8 could succeed the current 40mm and 25mm guns, improving supportability since while the latter two are unique to the AC-130, the former is used on other USAF types. The accuracy of the 105 mm gun may also be improved and countermeasures upgraded. Later data linking will be updated.

AC-130-UAV integration will continue to be improved. Four new, better-armed AC-130s will enter service in early 2006. In the longer term the AC-130 may eventually be replaced by one of a number of radical gunship concepts under study. The design could be stealthy and could be armed with lasers and other innovative weapons. Interoperability with UAVs would also be emphasized.

Specification:
First flight: 20 December 1990 (AC-130U)
Current users: US
Crew: Fourteen (AC-130H); thirteen (AC-130U)
Wing span: 40.4 m
Length: 19.8 m
Height: 11.7 m
Max take-off weight: 69,750 kg
Maximum speed: Mach 0.4 at sea level
Service ceiling: 7,576 m
Maximum range: 2,409 km

The Joint Strike Fighter (JSF) began as the Common Affordable Lightweight Fighter (CALF) programme of 1990. The Lockheed Martin contenders were designated X-35A (CTOL for USAF), X-35B (STOVL for USMC/RN) and X-35C (CV for USN). The X-35A first flew on 24 October 2000 followed by the -B and -C variants over the next ten months. On 26 October 2001, Lockheed Martin (with Northrop Grumman and BAe Systems) was selected to proceed to the $25 billion SDD phase, defeating a Boeing team in an industry fly-off. The F-35 operational derivative, which is to fly in late 2005, will have minor changes compared to the X-35.

The stealthy F-35 has a trapezoidal wing and tail and side-mounted air intakes. Flight controls are power-by-wire, the first on an operational fighter. An APG-81 multi-mode synthetic aperture radar with an AESA and six fuselage-mounted imaging IR (IIR) sensors will contribute to the helmet-mounted display system (in place of a HUD) and there will also be a laser designator and integrated chaff/flare dispensers. The F-35 is particularly impressive in the level of integration of information processing among the various sensors and controls.

The aircraft will use a Pratt & Whitney F135 turbofan engine producing 155.70 kN of thrust military power, but also capable of reheat. The General Electric/Rolls-Royce F136 is an alternate engine. The F135 has a three bearing swivelling exhaust nozzle. In the F-35B this combines with a lift fan mounted aft of the cockpit to enable STOVL operations. Weight growth has been a recent concern, this being most severe for the F-35B.

Six AMRAAMs or combinations of AMRAAMs, 900 kg JDAMs or short-range AAMs can be carried in two internal weapons bays while the JSOW, other bombs/LGBs, ARMs, JASSM and other ASMs and fuel tanks can be mounted externally on four hardpoints. The aircraft also has a 27 mm cannon. Other missiles, including European types, are to be integrated, and further directed energy/laser weapons are being studied.

The USAF, USMC and USN respectively require 1,763 (F-35As to succeed F-16s and A-10s and complement the F-22), 609 (F-35Bs to replace AV-8B, Harrier IIPlus and F/A-18C/Ds) and 480 (F-35Cs to replace the F/A-18C/D and partner the F/A-18E/F) but production figures could drop. In early 2004 the USAF expressed interest in also acquiring STOVL aircraft for CAS. Delivery is planned to begin in 2008, starting with the USAF. The UK requires 150 F-35s for its Joint Combat Aircraft (JCA) requirement to replace Harriers and Sea Harriers. The F-35B has been selected to succeed the Sea Harrier need and perhaps 60 may be acquired. The other F-35s will replace the Harrier. Further F-35s could be purchased as part of the FOAS to succeed Tornado strike aircraft from 2017.

Australia, Canada, Denmark, Israel, Italy, the Netherlands, Norway, Singapore and Turkey have also joined the programme. Total programme value is estimated at $200 billion. Cost-effective and all-round, the F-35 will be an important element of Western and allied air forces in the coming decades.

Another view of the X-35A. Lockheed Martin

Specification: (F-35)
First flight: 24 October 2000 (X-35A)
Current users: Intended for the US,
   UK and others (see text)
Crew: Pilot

Wing span: 12.19 m
Length: 15.52 m
Empty weight: 11,033 kg (X-35A)
Max take-off weight: about 22,680 kg
Maximum speed: Mach 1.8

Maximum range: 1,000/1,330 km
   radius of action for USMC/USN
   missions respectively

The X-35B hovers demonstrating its main engine tilt-exhaust.
US Marine Corps

Side view of the F-117A. USAF

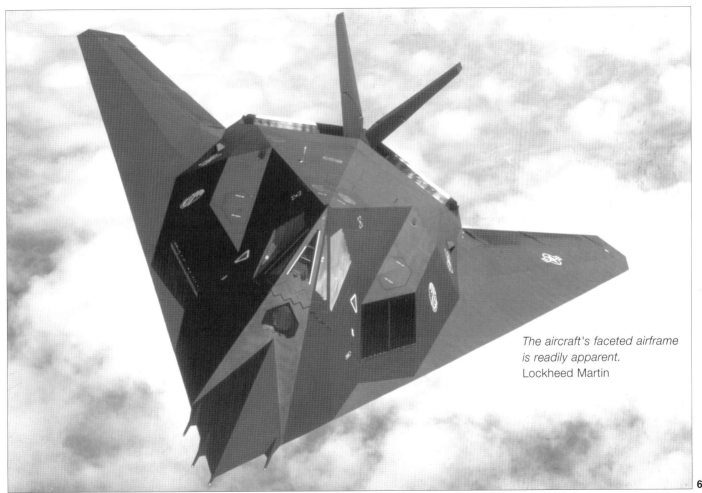

*The aircraft's faceted airframe
is readily apparent.*
Lockheed Martin

In 1975 Lockheed began studying a stealthy experimental aircraft the Have Blue. Development of a follow-on stealthy subsonic night attack aircraft, the F-117A, began in 1978 and first flight was achieved on 18 June 1981, although the type was only publicly revealed in 1988.

Its design is a lifting body with a swept delta wing and V-tail. Most unique though is the approach taken to confer stealth characteristics, the adoption of a faceted body with angular flat surfaces. Surfaces and edges reflect radar signals away from the radar detector while radar absorbent material (RAM) coated on the aircraft's surface contribute to a very low radar cross-section (RCS). The wing shields the engine inlets and combines with the tail to similarly protect the exhausts.

The F-117 does not have a radar but a FLIR and a downward-looking infrared (DLIR) with laser designator. There is also an infrared acquisition and designation system (IRADS). Two 47.04 kN-thrust General Electric F404-GE-F1D2 turbofans are used. Weapons could include the BLU-109B, GBU-10 and GBU-27 LGBs and Maverick and HARM ASMs and in the future JDAM.

The F-117A became the first operational stealth aircraft in the world, 59 aircraft entering USAF service. The only operator is the 49th Fighter Wing at Holloman AFB, New Mexico. These machines have been undergoing an upgrade to a Single Configuration Fleet, with work being done on the radar absorbent material and wing leading edge. GPS and a new INS have been installed and the computer modernised. The F-117A was not expected to remain in service for many years, and indeed under original plans replacement of the fleet would have already begun. However the aircraft now seems likely to remain in service to 2020 and beyond (although numbers could be reduced).

Specification:
First flight: 18 June 1981
Current users: US
Crew: Pilot
Wing span: 13.2 m
Length: 19.43 m
Height: 3.9 m
Empty weight: 13,393 kg
Max take-off weight: 23,800 kg

*Any view of the F-117 emphasizes
its unique shape.* USAF

Lockheed Martin Argentina IA-58A Pucara   Argentina

In the mid-1960s the Fabrica Militar de Aviones (Military Aircraft Factory), now Lockheed Martin Aircraft Argentina (LMAASA), began development of an aircraft for CAS, COIN and reconnaissance. The Pucara (stone fortress) which first flew on 20 August 1969 emerged as a two-crew, turboprop type.

The Pucara is rugged and simple and could operate from rough and forward airstrips, being easily supported in the field. Take-off run is 300m but this figure can be reduced by almost three-quarters by the use of rockets. The Pucara has an armoured cockpit floor and bulletproofed windshield. The cockpit has very good visibility. Night but not all-weather missions are possible. IA-58As use a pair of 730 kW Turboméca Aztazou XVIG turboprops. Maximum load of stores is 1,620 kg on five hardpoints (four underwing, one under the fuselage), weapons including GP, fragmentation and incendiary bombs, mines, torpedoes and Bullpup ASMs.

Additionally, the aircraft has a pair of Hispano-Suiza HS-804 20 mm cannon (with 270 rounds each) and four Browning 7.62 mm guns (900 rounds). The agile Pucara could also undertake air-to-air operations against helicopters and low-speed aircraft. Missions are often flown with a single crewmember.

Deliveries to the Argentine air force began in 1975. The air force received 108 aircraft in total, production ending in 1986. The Pucara has performed well against guerillas in Argentina. However the 1982 Falklands War revealed its shortcomings with 24 aircraft being lost, some of them captured, although it flew in missions it was not designed for. Aircraft were exported to Uruguay, Sri Lanka and Colombia but only in small numbers although an Iraqi request for 20 was refused. Argentine aircraft are being modernised by LMAASA with new avionics from 2004.

Specification:
First flight: 20 August 1969
Current users: Argentina, Colombia, Sri Lanka and Uruguay
Crew: Two
Wing span: 14.5 m
Length: 15.25 m
Height: 5.36 m
Empty weight: 4,037 kg
Max take-off weight: 6,800 kg
Max weapon load: 1,620 kg
Maximum speed: 500 km/h
Maximum range: 250 km radius on hi-lo-hi mission with maximum weapons and 10% fuel reserve; 3,042 km ferry range

An Argentine Pucara.
Rogier Westerhuis/Aero Image

LTV A-7 Corsair II

The A-7 was a proposal by Vought (now LTV) for a 1962 Navy requirement for a subsonic CAS aircraft. The aircraft was selected in February 1964 and its first flight made in September the following year.

The cost-effective A-7 was strong with a big weapons load, maintainable, accurate, long-ranged and simple to fly. Early models were the A-7A, B and C. Great improvements came with the A-7D and E including in particular to the avionics, weapons delivery and navigation systems. Apart from trainers, specialised night attack aircraft, the A-7D and K, were also produced. The YA-7F brought a supersonic capability but a production derivative did not enter service.

The A-7E has a 66.73 kN Allison TF-41-2 turbofan. 6,800 kg of weapons can be carried, which could include the Maverick, HARM and Shrike ASM/ARMs and a pair of Sidewinder AAMs. The aircraft also has a 20 mm Vulcan M61A-1 cannon.

From 1975 to 1977, Greece received fifty-nine single-seat A-7Hs and six two-seat TA-7Hs while a further thirty-six ex-US Navy A-7Es and TA-7Cs were also supplied in the 1990s. Eighty-nine A-7s remain in service. The first Greek aircraft flew on 6 May 1975, the nation becoming the first non-US customer. In Greek service the aircraft perform CAS, interdiction and maritime operations. Sidewinder AAMs provide a self-defence capability and also allow them to undertake air defence roles. The Greek air force is consolidating A-7 operations, reducing the number of units flying the type as the replacement F-16C/D Block 52+ enters service. The Royal Thai Navy obtained fourteen A-7E/EA-7Ls and four TA-7Cs from the US Navy in 1995 and these remain in service, operating from a land base.

Specification: (A-7E)
First flight: September 1965 (A-7)
Current users: Greece (TA-7C/A-7E/A-7H/TA-7H) and Thailand (TA-7C/A-7E/EA-7L)
Crew: Pilot; two for trainer versions
Wing span: 11.8 m
Length: 14.06 m
Height: 4.9 m
Empty weight: 8,668 kg
Max take-off weight: 19,050 kg
Max weapon load: 6,804 kg
Maximum speed: 1,112 km/h
Maximum range: 835 km radius on hi-lo-hi mission with 2,722 kg of bombs

An A-7 of the Royal Thai Navy.
Olaf Juergensmeier

McDonnell Douglas A-4 Skyhawk   USA

The A-4 was developed to meet a requirement for an aircraft-carrier-based attack aircraft. First flight was on 22 June 1954 and the aircraft remained in production until 1979.

Israel was by far the largest export customer and in all 350 A-4Hs, Fs and Es and TA-4H, were supplied between 1967 and 1973, although these have been upgraded to the A-4N standard. These aircraft undertake ground attack, EW support and training. Israel has delayed the planned withdrawal of its Skyhawks from 2005 to 2010 and as a result these aircraft are undergoing modernisation, including an upgrade to their avionics. Singapore has refurbished its aircraft to the A-4SU Super Skyhawk level, operational from 1988, with about sixty aircraft in service. The aircraft received new 48.93 kN-thrust General Electric F404-GE-100D turbofans which necessitated airframe structural improvements. Other systems including the cockpit and avionics were also upgraded.

Argentina was the first foreign customer of the aircraft, the first A-4s arriving in 1966. In 1994 Argentina ordered 36 ex-US A-4Ms. These were modernised to the A-4AR Fighting Hawk standard. The engine was refurbished and the new cockpit included a new radar, the ARG-1 (a development of the Northrop Grumman APG-66(V)), new avionics and displays, flight controls, navigational and weapons systems and HOTAS. In 1997 the Brazilian Navy obtained 23 upgraded ex-Kuwaiti T/A-4KUs. Further modernisation is possible including the fitting of a modern multi-mode radar and other avionics while the airframes could undergo a life extension. The first aircraft recovered on the aircraft carrier Minas Gerais on 18 January 2001.

Indonesia obtained its A-4Es in two batches, from Israel and from the US, the first delivery also including TA-4Hs. A further two TA-4Js were obtained from the US in 1999. An interesting new development is the commercial provision of adversary training for air forces. US-based ATSI has bought retired A-4s for this role.

Specification: (A-4SU)
First flight: 22 June 1954 (A-4)
Current users: Argentina (A-4AR/TA-4AR), Indonesia (A-4E/TA-4H/TA-4J), Israel (A-4N) and Singapore (A-4SU/TA-4SU)
Crew: Pilot; two for trainer versions.
Wing span: 8.38 m
Length: 12.7 m
Height: 4.57 m
Empty weight: 4,650 kg
Max take-off weight: 10,200 kg
Maximum speed: 1,128 km/h
Maximum rate of climb: 3,325 m per minute
Service ceiling: 12,190 m
Maximum range: 1,160 km

An A-4SU of the Republic of Singapore Air Force. George Canciani

71

Mitsubishi F-1 Japan

The F-1 is a CAS and maritime strike aircraft derived from the T-2 trainer. Development began in 1972 and the F-1 first flew on 3 June 1975. After successful evaluation with the JASDF, the first production aircraft flew in 1977. Seventy-seven aircraft were produced in total with the last in 1986, but the aircraft now only equips one JASDF squadron.

There is a high degree of commonality between the F-1 and the T-2; the aircraft structure is the same and the F-1 retains the trainer's pair of licence-built 31.45 kN-thrust Ishikawajima-Harima TF40-IHI-801A turbofans. Avionics includes an AWG-12 multi-mode radar, fire control system and RHAWS. Some avionics, including a weapon-aiming computer and INS, and extra fuel, occupy the space that was used by the second cockpit in the T-2.

Four underwing weapons pylons, which could also use multiple ejector racks, could carry a 2,722 kg payload including bombs, rocket pods, ASM-1 anti-ship missile. Up to four Sidewinder or AAM-1 AAMs could be carried including on the wingtips. There is also a 20 mm JM-61 cannon. A centreline fuselage and two underwing hardpoints could carry fuel tanks. Combat radius is limited though; with a 1,800 kg weapons load and tanks radius is only 350 km. Commonality with the T-2 makes conversion from that aircraft easy.

Specification:
First flight: 3 June 1975
Current users: Japan
Crew: Pilot (F-1); two (T-2)
Wing span: 7.87 m
Length: 17.86 m
Height: 4.39 m
Empty weight: 6,358 kg
Max take-off weight: 13,701 kg
Max weapon load: 2,722 kg
Maximum speed: Mach 1.6
Maximum rate of climb: 10,670 m per minute
Service ceiling: 15,250 m
Maximum range: 1,126 m with eight 227 kg bombs

Camouflaged JASDF F-1.
Jaroslaw Zaczek

Mitsubishi F-2 — Japan

The F-2 was developed (as the FS-X initially) as a replacement for the JASDF's F-1 aircraft in the close air support and anti-ship roles. The project was agreed upon on October 1987 and Japanese/US production work sharing arranged the following year. Development began in 1990. Political factors (the requirement for the aircraft to be based on a US type and the need for US companies to have extensive involvement) contributed to the F-2 being considerably more expensive (the cost is estimated at $100 million) than the latest variants of the F-16 (the aircraft on which the F-2 design is based) and more expensive even than new generation combat aircraft. The aircraft first flew on 7 October 1995. Wing structural problems delayed flight testing resulting in the first aircraft being delivered to the JASDF on 26 September 2000 and IOC being achieved the following year.

The F-16 ancestry is clearly evident but the F-2 has a bigger and differently shaped wing and tailplane, the former providing 25 % more area. It also has a longer forward and centre fuselage, shorter jet exhaust pipe and reinforced windshield. An indigenous active phased array look-down/shoot-down radar, the first such type on a production warplane, allows simultaneous air and ground target tracking. Other avionics and systems are primarily Japanese. Advanced composites are used in the structure. The F-2 is powered by a General Electric F110-GE-129 turbofan capable of 131.67 kN with afterburning and built locally by IAI.

Maximum payload is 9,527 kg including Japanese and US general-purpose, laser-guided and cluster bombs, rocket launchers and AAMs including the Mitsubishi AAM-3 while JDAM will also be introduced. Weapons are deployed on 13 stations including a pair of wingtip AAM rails. A port wing-root-mounted 20 mm M61A1 Vulcan cannon. A representative maritime strike loadout is four indigenous ASM-2 anti-ship missiles.

130 are being built for the JASDF comprising eighty-three single-seat F-2As and forty-seven two-seat F-2B operational trainers, the F-2As equipping three combat wings at Misawa and Tsuiki, with the last aircraft to be delivered in 2007. An air superiority version has been proposed while the F-2B could replace the current T-2/A advanced trainers.

Specification:
First flight: 7 October 1995
Current users: Japan
Crew: Pilot (F-2A); two (F-2B)
Wing span: 11.13 m with wingtip missile rails
Length: 15.52 m
Height: 4.96 m
Empty weight: 9,527 kg (F-2A)
Max take-off weight: 20,517 kg with two AAMs, four anti-ship missiles and two drop tanks
Max weapon load: 8,085-9,000 kg
Maximum speed: Mach 2 at altitude
Maximum range: More than 830 km combat radius for anti-ship missions

The Mitsubishi F-2.
Lockheed Martin

An armed A-10A. USAF

A view of the A-10 showing
its array of weapons.
USAF

In 1967, the USAF promulgated a requirement for a dedicated CAS aircraft that could deploy a substantial payload of anti-armour and other weapons from short, undeveloped forward bases, was simple, survivable, reliable and maintainable, had long range and high endurance and manoeuvrability and was affordable. Not surprisingly, the aircraft that emerged to fulfil this need, the A-10, was quite unlike its fighter contemporaries. It was large, comparable in size to a WWII bomber, had a long, unswept wing and tail and two engines mounted in pods high on the rear fuselage. The YA-10A prototype first flew on 10 May 1972 and in all 713 aircraft were built for the USAF. However, only about half of this number remain in service, attrition being particularly severe. Apart from the standard A-10A, many of the USAF's aircraft are designated OA-10A for FAC.

The pilot has a good all-round view from the Night Vision Imaging System-compatible cockpit but avionics fit is basic. Titanium cockpit armour offers protection from 23 mm calibre ammunition and survivability is further enhanced by the use of hydraulic flight controls with manual backup and of foam-protected self-sealing fuel tanks among other redundant components. The aircraft can withstand a high degree of combat damage. Power is provided by a pair of 40.32 kN General Electric TF34-GE-100 turbofan engines.

The A-10 has a 30 mm GAU-8/A Avenger seven-barrel Gatling gun, the most powerful gun ever fitted on a tactical combat aircraft, capable of firing at 4,200 rounds per minute. Eleven hardpoints can carry up to 7,257 kg of weapons and stores including the Maverick missile. The Litening II targeting pod enables day/night delivery of laser-guided weapons, such as those used in Operation Iraqi Freedom in 2003.

The A-10 was designed to operate at low level below hostile radar. However, since Operation Allied Force in Kosovo in 1999, operations have been increasingly occurring at medium altitude with longer-range weapons, the gun also being successfully used at medium level in these operations. Further, the aircraft, unlike most other fixed-wing attack jets, could operate from under-developed forward operating locations.

Under the Precision Engagement programme the aircraft are receiving a digital weapons management system, 1760 weapons data bus and new data links. The aircraft will also be fitted with the TERPROM Digital Terrain System (DTS), Embedded GPS/INU, new countermeasures suite, the Comet IR countermeasures pod and a targeting pod. JDAM and WCMD are to be integrated. In early 2004 the USAF revealed its interest in re-engining of and further upgrades for the A-10s.

The A-10 is planned to remain in service to at least 2028 when it will be replaced by the JSF.

Head-on view of a pair of A-10s in formation. USAF

Specification:
First flight: 10 May 1972
Current users: US
Crew: Pilot
Wing span: 17.53 m
Length: 16.26 m
Height: 4.47 m
Empty weight: 9,761 kg
Max take-off weight: 22,680 kg
Max weapon load: 7,257 kg
Maximum speed: 681 km/h
Maximum rate of climb: 1,828 m per
  minute at a weight of 14,420 kg
Maximum range: 463 km with 1.8h
  loiter and fuel reserve; 1,000 km
  radius for deep strike; 4,091 km
  ferry range

Northrop Grumman B-2A Spirit

USA

The unique B-2A of the USAF.
USAF

80

In 1974, the US Defence Advanced Research Projects Agency began studying stealth aircraft technologies. In 1980, a new long-range bomber requirement was promulgated, this eventually becoming the Advanced Technology Bomber (ATB). Northrop secured the contract in October 1981 with its subsonic flying-wing design, to be designated the B-2A. At first, the aim was to produce a high altitude bomber but in 1983 the operational profile was changed to include low-level operations. The B-2A first flew on 17 July 1989.

The B-2A uses the low-probability-of-intercept AN/APG-181 radar which has twenty-one modes. The aircraft is powered by four General Electric F118-GE-100 non-afterburning turbofans, each capable of producing 84.518 kN of thrust. The B-2A shares the strategic nuclear bombing role with the B-52 but only the B-2 would actually fly over enemy territory (the B-52 operating in a standoff role). The two centre-fuselage bomb bays could accommodate 18,145 kg of weapons which could include the B61-7, B61-11 and B83 Mod 0 nuclear bombs.

Another view of the B-2. USAF

Close-up of the B-2's nose.
Gerhard Plomitzer

The B-2A has a two-man crew (two pilots) but a third crewmember could also be supported. The USAF's aircraft cost $2 billion apiece.

In December 1983, the USAF 509th Bomb Wing received the first production aircraft, Block 10. These were followed by Block 20 and Block 30 aircraft. All twenty-one aircraft (reduced from the initially planned 132) were in service by 1998 and the earlier examples were brought to the Block 30 level. The radar-absorbent material, which was susceptible to moisture, has been improved in Block 30 aircraft. Aircraft edges have been refinished, surface coatings replaced and the armament range expanded. The late-block B-2 could also carry JDAM, cluster bombs, mines, free-fall bombs and other weapons.

The B-2 was first operationally used in Operation Allied Force against Yugoslavia in 1999. They flew from the force's home base at Whiteman AFB in Missouri in what was the first extensive offensive air strikes from the continental US. The 49 sorties represented only 3 % of the combat effort but struck 39 % of the targets.

Aircrew are in fact trained for 50-hour sorties with a B-2 setting a combat mission record of 44.3 hours during Operation Enduring Force against Afghanistan in 2001-2002 (30-hour sorties being achieved in Allied Force). However the length of the roundtrip severely limited B-2 Enduring Freedom missions and the USAF has been constructing specialised facilities at overseas locations. The B-2 still is hampered by slow speed and once seen has little defences against fighter aircraft. Stealth maintenance has also been problematic, contributing to the aircraft's low mission capable rate; there have also been structural problems.

Northrop Grumman is integrating an AESA with the existing radar, enabling radar range and resolution to increase. The new radar will function at a different frequency to prevent interference with commercial users. Beyond-line-of-sight (BLOS) communications and a Multifunction Information Distribution System (MIDS)/Link-16 datalink capability are being fitted. Further possible improvements are to the computer, data bus, controls and displays. New and updated weapons including JDAM, the GPS/laser-guided GBU-28B/B bomb, AGM-158 standoff missile and JASSM are being integrated or evaluated and data links updated; in tests a B-2 has dropped 80 JDAMs on 80 separate targets.

Specification:
First flight: 17 July 1989
Current users: US
Crew: Two
Wing span: 52.43 m
Length: 21.03 m
Height: 5.18 m
Empty weight: 56,700-69,715 kg
Max take-off weight: 152,633 kg
Max weapon load: 18,145 kg
Maximum speed: Mach 0.8
Maximum rate of climb: 915 m per minute at sea level at 125,644 kg weight
Service ceiling: 15,240 m
Maximum range: 11,110 km range with a 14,515 kg payload at high altitude

A pair of German Tornado IDS aircraft.
EADS

A Tornado ECR with four HARM weapons. EADS

The Tornado is the result of a tri-national European programme for an interdiction/strike (IDS) aircraft. It is configured as a compact, two-seat, twin-engined VG design. The prototype first flew on 14 August 1974. An electronic combat and reconnaissance (ECR) version was later developed. 780 IDS/ECR aircraft were produced for the European partners, the UK (228 IDS), Germany (air force 210 IDS and thirty-five ECR, and navy 112 IDS) and Italy (ninety-nine IDS with fifteen later converted to ECR standard) and for Saudi Arabia (ninety-six IDS), production ending in 1998 with the last aircraft supplied to Saudi Arabia.

Tornado has a multi-mode Ground Mapping Radar, TFR and doppler navigation radar. Avionics are integrated by a 1553B data bus. 142 of the RAF's attack/reconnaissance GR.Mk1/1As have been modernised to the GR.Mk4/4A standard followed by the maritime strike GR1B. The first upgraded GR Mk.4 flew on 4 April 1997, the aircraft becoming operational in April 1998. The GR.Mk4/4As have FLIR, NVG-compatible cockpit, new displays, a new 1760 weapons bus, HOTAS (fitted later), Terprom terrain reference navigation system, secure radio, GPS and updated EW. Other and future RAF upgrades are a new main computer, further display improvements, updated IFF system, data links and collision warning system, EW upgrade and structural strengthening. German and Italian aircraft are also receiving an MLU. They are getting a data bus, new computer, updated sensors and displays, GPS/INS, FLIR, and improved IFF and EW/self-defence systems. Improved night capability is to follow. Each of the pair of Turbo Union RB199 Mk103(Mk105) turbofans produces 71.2 kN(74.3 kN) of thrust with reheat.

The IDS can carry 9,000 kg of stores including a very comprehensive array of free-fall, retarded, low-drag, cluster, and laser-guided bombs (including Paveway III), rocket pods, weapon dispensers and Maverick, anti-ship Kormoran and anti-radiation ALARM and HARM and other missiles with the Sidewinder AAM for self-defence. Two 25 mm Mauser cannon are mounted on the sides of the lower fuselage. The RAF ordered the IPGB after the Balkan operations but more recently the service's aircraft have been integrating the standoff Storm Shadow and anti-armour Brimstone. RAF Tornadoes operationally evaluated the Storm Shadow (before it was in squadron use) and also employed the Enhanced Paveway LGB over Iraq in early 2003. In addition, RAF aircraft will be able to use the modernized ALARM. German and Italian Tornadoes returning from their MLUs will be able to launch Paveway III, HARM III, Storm Shadow and other weapons. JDAM and JSOW are future IDS options. Other stores include TIALD (RAF GR.Mk4/4As) and other laser-designating pods (Litening for German/Italian MLU aircraft), recon pods (including RAPTOR for the RAF), ECM pods, chaff/flare dispensers and fuel tanks.

ECR Tornadoes have an EW package (in place of the gun), a wing-root-mounted threat radar emitter locator, imaging IR linescan, ODIN data link, FLIR and HARM. These aircraft are receiving the same MLU as their IDS counterparts. With the MLUs, Tornadoes have many years of service ahead. RAF aircraft in particular are planned to remain in service to 2018-20 when replaced by the FOAS.

Specification:
First flight: 4 August 1974
Current users: Germany (IDS/ECR), Italy (IDS/ECR), Saudi Arabia (IDS) and the UK (IDS)
Crew: Two
Wing span: 13.91 m spread; 8.6 m swept
Length: 16.7 m with probe
Height: 5.95 m
Empty weight: 14,000 kg
Max take-off weight: 28,000 kg
Max weapon load: 9,000 kg
Maximum speed: Mach 2.2 clean; Mach 1.8 with stores
Service ceiling: Above 15,240 m
Maximum range: 1,482 km radius on hi-lo-hi interdiction mission with four 454 kg bombs, two AAMs and two drop tanks; 3,797 km ferry range

Another German Tornado ECR. EADS

Rockwell OV-10 Bronco

The OV-10 was selected to meet the US's Light Armed Reconnaissance Airplane (LARA) COIN requirement, the aircraft first flying on 16 July 1965. The pod and twin-boom OV-10 was optimised for rough field operations. Seven hardpoints, four on the sponsons, one centreline and two under the wing, enable the carriage of rocket launchers, missiles, a gun pod or a fuel tank, to a weight of 1,633 kg. Four 7.62 mm guns are fitted in the sponsons. OV-10s currently in service use two 533kW Garett AiResearch T76-G-416/417 turboprops.

The USMC was an enthusiastic OV-10 operator using the aircraft for FAC, light attack and related roles. The Marines also flew the most capable Bronco, the OV-10D, with more powerful engines, FLIR, and chaff/flare dispensers, this aircraft performing well in Operation Desert Storm against Iraq in 1991. The USAF and USN also used OV-10s.

Colombia has OV-10As, to be replaced. Indonesia received 12 OV-10Fs, which are overhauled OV-10As, these having their M60C guns replaced with 12.7 mm M2 Browning weapons. The Philippines' squadron of OV-10Cs has flown in anti-terrorist operations and is among that country's most important air attack forces. Numbers are being boosted by ex-Thai aircraft, the latter now retiring its force of OV-10Cs. Some of the Thai aircraft also use 12.7 mm machine guns instead of M60Cs. Venezuela originally received 16 OV-10Es. They were commandeered and used by anti-government rebels in 1993, three being shot down by opposing loyalist forces. Venezuelan OV-10s have also operated against Colombian-based rebels.

Specification: (OV-10A)
First flight: 16 July 1965
Current users: Colombia (OV-10A), Indonesia (OV-10F), The Philippines (OV-10C), Thailand (OV-10C) and Venezuela (OV-10E)
Crew: Two
Wing span: 12.19 m
Length: 12.67 m
Height: 4.62 m
Empty weight: 3,127 kg
Max take-off weight: 6,552 kg
Max weapon load: 1,633 kg
Maximum speed: 452 km/h
Maximum range: 367 km with maximum weapons; 2,224 km ferry range with maximum fuel

An OV-10 of the Royal Thai Air Force. Erik Frikke

RSK MiG-17 & Shenyang J-5 "Fagot" Russia/China

The MiG-15 was the Soviet fighter that gave US pilots a shock in the Korean War of 1950-53. This aircraft was entirely reworked to become the MiG-17, the prototype of which first flew on 13 January 1950.

The MiG-17 was able to achieve Mach 1 in tests but operational aircraft were subsonic being powered by a 33.03 kN-thrust afterburning Klimov VK-1A turbojet in the case of the major model, the MiG-17F. The radar-equipped MiG-17PF introduced all-weather capability. The aircraft was for many years the standard export fighter for Soviet clients and production occurred in China, Czechoslovakia and Poland, some of these aircraft also being delivered to other countries. Chinese J-5/J-5As, based on the MiG-17PF, use a Wopen-built Klimov engine and China also developed its own two-seat JJ-5 model built by Chengdu. Chinese exports were known as F-5 and FT-5 respectively. Shenyang also produced MiG-17F-derived J-4s.

The MiG-17 was able to out-fly US aircraft it faced in the Vietnam War (although better US training balanced the equation) but its time as a fighter has long passed. It is a strong, well-designed aircraft and although this enabled it to remain in service for many years in a number of air forces in attack roles it is now also thoroughly obsolete in that capacity. China has a large force on paper (estimated at 600 J-5/J-5As, 350 J-4s and 500 JJ-5s) for attack and training but the operational readiness of the fleet must be questionable. North Korea also has large numbers of F-5s.

Armament comprised one 37 mm and two 23 mm cannon or three of the latter while additionally the four underwing hardpoints could carry rocket pods and bombs.

Specification:
First flight: 13 January 1950
Current users: Albania (F-5/FT-5), Congo, Cuba, Ethiopia, Guinea, Guinea-Bissau, Madagascar, North Korea (F-5/FT-5), Sri Lanka (FT-5) and Syria. Includes aircraft used as trainers
Crew: Pilot; two for trainer versions
Wing span: 9.6 m
Length: 11.36 m
Height: 3.8 m
Max take-off weight: 5,340 kg
Max weapon load: 500 kg
Maximum speed: 1,145 km/h
Maximum rate of climb: 3,900 m per minute
Service ceiling: 16,500 m
Maximum range: 1,340 km

A former North Korean MiG-17 acquired by the USAF.
Neil C Martin

A Sri Lankan Air Force MiG-27. Rogier Westerhuis/Aero Image

The MiG-23BN (Flogger-H) was developed from the MiG-23 fighter series and its airframe resembles that of its immediate production predecessor sub-type, the MiG-23B. The MiG-23BN however has been strengthened for the low-level environment while other changes are the RWR antennae mounted on the lower fuselage ahead of the engine intakes and a missile guidance antenna faired onto the starboard wing glove. Power is provided by a 51.15 kN Turmanskii R-29 engine. The MiG-23BN was primarily an export aircraft and a number of Warsaw Pact states and Third World nations received the type. Small numbers also served with the Soviet air forces.

The ground attack capabilities were refined further in the MiG-27 (Flogger-D), initially known as the MiG-23BM, which in fact flew before the MiG-23BN, on 17 November 1972. The MiG-27 became operational in February 1975. The most visible difference from the MiG-23BN are the simplified engine inlets which resulted in maximum speed dropping from Mach 2.35 to Mach 1.7. The MiG-27 also has a different gun, the GSh-6-30 30 mm while weapons stations were able to carry heavier loads, the total payload growing to 4,000 kg. The MiG-27K (Flogger-J2, initially MiG-23BK) first flew on 30 December 1974. It had a new laser/TV designation system to enable the use of laser-guided weapons. Capable but expensive, only limited numbers joined the Soviet air forces from 1980. The MiG-27M (Flogger-J), which first flew in April 1976, was a simplified model. It saw greater use with the Soviet air arms and additionally Flogger-Ds were upgraded to the Flogger-J standard, being designated MiG-27D.

India licence-built its own MiG-27 version, 165 aircraft emerging from the HAL production line between 1986 and 1994. A development of the MiG-27M with some indigenous systems, these aircraft were designated MiG-27L (by the Russians but MiG-27M by the Indians). India has more than 130 aircraft which are to be modernised. Sri Lanka received a few ex-Ukrainian MiG-27Ms and these have been active in the counterinsurgency against the LTTE terrorists.

Withdrawing forces at the end of the Cold War, the Russians decided to retain dual-engined types and the MiG-23BNs/27s in the main formed a reserve. They are still capable aircraft and are available for sale to international customers, with upgrades being offered by Russian organizations.

Specification:
First flight: 17 November 1972 (MIG-27)
Current users: Algeria (MiG-23BN), Bulgaria (MiG-23BN), Cuba (MiG-23BN), Ethiopia (MiG-23BN), India (MiG-23BN, MiG-27M), Iraq (MiG-23BN), Libya (MiG-23BN), Russia (MiG-27, stored), Sri Lanka (MiG-27M/UB), Syria (MiG-23BN) and Yemen (MiG-23BN). Includes aircraft used as trainers.
Crew: Pilot; two for trainer versions.
Wing span: 13.97 m spread; 7.78 m swept
Length: 17.08 m
Height: 5 m
Empty weight: 12,100 kg
Max take-off weight: 20,670 kg
Max weapon load: 4,000 kg
Maximum speed: Mach 1.7
Maximum rate of climb: 12,000 m per minute
Service ceiling: 14,000 m
Maximum range: 2,500 km with three drop tanks

The Jaguar emerged to fulfil an Anglo-French requirement for an advanced training and light attack aircraft with the latter need becoming more important as the programme progressed and as the capability of the aircraft was revealed. Based on the French Breguet Br 121 design, the Jaguar first flew on 8 September 1968. The aircraft has proven to be reliable, rugged, maintainable and durable with good performance.

RAF Jaguars have been updated to the GR.Mk.3/3A standard with TIALD, improved navigation

A French Air Force Jaguar.
Dassault Aviation

An RAF Jaguar in reheat.
Damien Burke

systems, NVG-compatible cockpits, MIL-STD-1553B data bus, Terprom ground warning system and GPS. A helmet mounted sighting system (HMSS) is the latest modification. Trainers have been upgraded to the corresponding T.Mk.4 standard. The aircraft are also being re-engined with Adour Mk 106s instead of the problematic MK 104s, the new powerplant providing 36.69 kN of thrust with afterburning.

The French single- and two-seat aircraft are known respectively as the Jaguar A and E.

French single-seat Jaguar As have the Atlis II target TV acquisition- and laser-designation pod to enable the use of precision weapons. Apart from free-fall bombs and cluster bombs, anti-runway and area-denial submunitions, AS30L ASMs and LGBs, tactical nuclear weapons are also in its arsenal. British and French aircraft have seen combat in Africa (French machines), the Middle East and the former Yugoslavia.

The Jaguar entered service in India, where it is known as the Shamsher (Sword), to fulfil an IAF long-range strike requirement. India is the largest operator of the aircraft and indeed, although production in Europe ended in 1985, it continues in that country with the IAF to eventually receive a total of 168 aircraft. IAF aircraft have had Elta EL/M-2032 radar installed. They have also been fitted with the DARIN (Display Attack and Ranging Inertial and Navigation) system which includes INS, HUDWAC, a new autopilot, 'smart' MFD and LRMTS. Further modern Line Replacement Units have replaced old gyros and computers. The latest batch of Jaguars, being equipped with DARIN, will be able to use laser-guided weapons and be more capable in night attack. Shamshers use a pair of Rolls Royce/Turbomeca Adourt Mk811 turbofans, each of which provides 37.4 kN of thrust with afterburner. Most of the IAF's Jaguars perform land attack and some may be configured for nuclear carriage. The service also has a maritime attack squadron with radar-equipped

aircraft that use the Sea Eagle missile. Omani Jaguars have also received an avionics update.

RAF aircraft will remain in service to at least 2008 but elsewhere the Jaguar will be operational for many more years, at least with the IAF.

Specification:
First flight: 8 September 1968
Current users: Ecuador (ES/EB),
  France (A/E), India (IS/IM/IB),
  Nigeria (SN/BN), Oman (S/B) and
  the UK GR3/3A/T4)
Crew: Pilot; two for trainer versions.
Wing span: 8.69 m
Length: 16.83 m

Height: 4.89 m
Empty weight: 7,000 kg
Max take-off weight: 15,700 kg
Max weapon load: 4,763 kg
Maximum speed: Mach 1.6
Maximum range: 852 km radius on
  hi-lo-hi mission with weapons;
  4,210 km ferry range

Another RAF Jaguar.
Damien Burke

SOKO J-1 Jastreb and UTVA G-4 Super Galeb

former Yugoslavia/Serbia

A camouflaged Jastreb of the Republika Sprska Air Force.
Salinger Igor

The G-2 Galeb (Seagull) trainer, the first Yugoslav jet aircraft, made its maiden flight in May 1961. Apart from a sole Serbian aircraft that survived the 1999 NATO air campaign against Yugoslavia, the only current user is Libya. Combat capability was emphasized in the development of the Galeb but a specialised single-seat attack version was produced as the J-1 Jastreb (Hawk, designated J-21 by the Yugoslav forces), first flight occurring in 1967. Improvements included a strengthened airframe with the second cockpit faired over, a more powerful engine, the 13.34 kN-thrust Rolls Royce Viper 531 (with JATO rockets optional for take-off) and new communications and navigation systems. The Jastreb has three nose-mounted 12.7 mm guns and eight underwing pylons for 800 kg of stores. The RJ-1 reconnaissance variant had fuselage and wingtip cameras but only four underwing hardpoints for a smaller weapons load than the basic Jastreb. A trainer model, the TJ-1, was also produced. Small numbers of Jastrebs remain in the Republika Sprska order of battle but Serbia has retired its

aircraft. J-1s and RJ-1s, designated J-1Es and RJ-1Es, were also exported to Libya and Zambia.

The replacement for the G-2, the G-4 Super Galeb (military designation N-62), first flew on 17 July 1978. The redesigned fuselage featured stepped cockpits, power being provided by the 17.79 kN-thrust Viper 632. A 23 mm GSh-23L twin-barrel cannon was installed under the fuselage while stores carried on the four underwing hardpoints could include AAMs, bombs/bomb dispensers, napalm, rockets/rocket pods, fuel tanks and ECM pods. Deliveries occurred throughout the 1980s and aircraft were being refurbished when the allied air campaign was launched. Serbia has more than a squadron's-worth of Super Galebs for training and attack, while a single Sprskan aircraft survived the civil war in Bosnia and Herzegovina.

A programme to improve the combat capability of the Super Galeb was begun in the early 1990s but the Yugoslav conflicts adversely affected progress and the G-4M prototype only first flew on March 22, 1999. As a result also of the conflict the G-4

project was transferred from SOKO to UTVA. The G-4M has an improved nav/attack, HOTAS and a new HUD. The aircraft could use Maverick ASMs and wing-tip R-60 AAMs with its seven weapons stations able to carry a 1950 kg payload.

Specification (J-1):
First flight: 1967 (J-1) and 17 July 1978 (G-4)
Current users: Libya (J-1), Republika Sprska (J-1, G-4), Serbia (G-4) and Zambia (J-1)
Crew: Pilot (J-1); two (G-4)
Wing span: 11.68 m with wingtip tanks
Length: 10.88 m
Height: 3.64 m
Empty weight: 2,820 kg
Max take-off weight: 5,100 kg
Max weapon load: 800 kg
Maximum speed: 820 km/h
Maximum rate of climb: 1,260 m per minute at sea level
Service ceiling: 12,000 m
Maximum range: 9,000 m with full wingtip tanks

The variable-geometry Su-17/20/22 family of VG attack aircraft has its origins in the swept-wing Su-7. In 1965, Sukhoi began working on improving the airfield performance of the Su-7, then Soviet FA's primary attack type and the S-22I, featuring outer-wing variable sweep, made its maiden flight on 2 August 1966. The aircraft entered service as the Su-17 (NATO codename Fitter-B) with improved avionics. This was followed by the Su-17M Fitter-C which boasted better performance on the strength of a new engine. Around this time Sukhoi was also producing the export Su-20 (Fitter-C) with less sophisticated avionics and the older engine but which still was the first version able to fire AAMs. The Su-20 first flew in December 1972.

The Su-17M2 Fitter-D had improved avionics and was able to field the latest Soviet weapons. This aircraft was also exported, as the Su-22 (Fitter-F), again with downgraded systems. It used the Turmanskii R29BS-300 turbojet capable of 112.27 kN with afterburner. The Su-22 was built from 1976 to 1980. The single-seat Su-17M3 (Fitter-H) developed from the Su-17UM trainer had substantially improved nav/attack capability and new weapons to allow it to undertake SEAD missions. The downgraded Su-17M was the export model. Su-17UM trainers, when fitted with Su-17UM systems, were re-designated Su-17UM3, with the Su-22UM3K being the export counterpart. The Su-17M4 (Fitter-K) featured digital avionics, the corresponding export Su-22M4 using the 109.82 kN Lyulka AL-21F-3 engine. The Su-22M4, produced from 1984 to1990, was the ultimate export Fitter. The Su-22's load of air-to-ground weapons was supplemented by its two wing-root 30 mm guns. The aircraft could also carry reconnaissance stores.

The navigation and communication systems of Poland's Su-22M4 and Su-22UM3Ks were modernised to improve NATO interoperability but the country further has evaluated the use of an adapter kit that allows unguided weapons to be guided. Poland is to receive spares from Sukhoi after a twelve year break and this would enable to reach their expected retirement date of 2010-2012. Peruvian aircraft were upgraded with Western systems.

Specification: (Su-22M4)

First flight: 2 August 1966 (S-22I); December 1972 (Su-20)

Current users: Angola (Su-22M4/ Azerbaijan (Su-17M), Bulgaria (Su-22M/U), Iran (Su-20/22), Iraq (Su-7/20/22), Libya (Su-20/22/22M3), Peru (Su-20/Su-22M/U), Poland (Su-22M4/Su-22UM3), Slovakia (Su-22M4/U), Syria (Su-22M/U), Ukraine (Su-17M/UM), Uzbekistan (Su-17M/UB), Vietnam (Su-22) and Yemen (Su-22BKL/M2/U). Includes aircraft used as trainers

Crew: Pilot; two for trainer versions

Wing span: 13.8 m spread; 10.0 m swept

Length: 19.13 m

Max take-off weight: 19,500 kg

Max weapon load: 4,250 kg

Maximum speed: Mach 2.09

Service ceiling: 15,210 m

Sukhoi Su-24 "Fencer"

A camouflaged and armed Russian Su-24M at base.
Hugo Mambour/AviaScribe

The Sukhoi Su-24 is a nuclear-capable tactical strike aircraft that can also undertake reconnaissance and EW. Its origin can be traced to a 1961 requirement to replace the Yak-28 attack aircraft. Sukhoi was influenced by the US success with the F-111 VG strike platform and on 17 January 1970, the T6-2IG VG prototype first flew. Series production began the following year, the

aircraft achieving IOC in 1974.

Power is provided by a pair of Saturn AL-21F-3 turbojet engines each producing 109.8kN of thrust with reheat. Fencer-C, the main initial variant, was followed by the upgraded Su-24M (Fencer-D), the EW Su-24MP (Fencer-F) and the Su-24MR (Fencer-E). Fencer-D offered significant combat improvement over the earlier models and its eight hardpoints could

dispense 8,000 kg of stores (Fencer-A, -B and -C being restricted to 7,000 kg). These could include tactical nuclear bombs but additionally the aircraft could carry a wide array of conventional weapons including anti-radiation, laser- and TV-guided missiles, bombs, submunitions dispensers and rockets. Fencer-E and -F are unarmed.

An update of the Su-24M to Su-24M2

(Above) *An Su-24M2 takes off.* Hugo Mambour/AviaScribe
(Below) *A pair of Su-24Ms taxiing.* Hugo Mambour/AviaScribe

standard by Gefest and T is being evaluated by the Russian air force. Apart from upgraded navigation/computer systems, possibly including GPS, and modernised displays, the aircraft will be able to deliver a wider range of precision guided weapons now including the KH-29L, Kh-31P anti-radiation and Kh-59M ASMs.

With the break-up of the USSR, the Soviet fleet was re-distributed and in addition to Russia, the Ukraine, Belarus, Kazakhstan and Azerbaijan obtained Su-24s. Algeria received an initial batch of thirteen and also a further twenty-two upgraded ex-Russian Su-24MKs (similar to Su-24Ms). Algeria's aircraft are expected to undergo the Sukhoi Combat Enhancement Capability Improvement (CECI) update. Iran also obtained Su-24s, including some from another customer, Iraq, held as war reparations. Syria and Libya are the remaining recipients.

Specification (Su-24M):
First flight: 17 January 1970 (T6-2IG)
Current users: Algeria (Su-24/MR), Azerbaijan, Belarus (Su-24MK/MR), Iran (Su-24MK), Kazakhstan, Libya (Su-24MK), Russia (Su-24/MR/MP), Syria (Su-24MK) and Ukraine (Su-24M/MR/MP) and Uzbekistan (Su-24/MR)
Crew: Two
Wing span: 17.64 m spread;10.37 m fully swept
Length: 24.53 m
Height: 6.19 m
Empty weight: 22,320 kg
Max take-off weight: 39,700 kg
Max weapon load: 8,000 kg
Maximum speed: Mach 1.35
Maximum range: 560 km radius at 200 m with drop tanks; 2,500 km range at high altitude with two 3,000 l drop tanks

(Above) *A Belarus Su-25UB trainer.*
Sergey Burdin

(Left) *Upgraded Su-25TM.*
Hugo Mambour/Aviascribe

In March 1969, the Soviet Air Force promulgated a requirement for a subsonic close air support aircraft for daylight, fair-weather operations. Later that year the T-8, the forerunner of the Su-25, was chosen to fulfil this need, development of the aircraft having begun in 1968. Maiden flight of the first prototype was on 22 February 1975. Two prototypes were evaluated in Afghanistan in 1980 and when the first operational unit formed the following year, its aircraft were also soon involved in that theatre.

The Su-25 was designed to be simple, tough and maintainable and able to withstand a lot of punishment, in particular its cockpit being armoured. These factors helped make it the most suitable aircraft for the conditions in Afghanistan, the aircraft's agility and payload additionally being well appreciated. It is powered by a pair of 40.21 kN-thrust Soyuz/Moscow R-95Sh non-afterburning turbojets. Total payload is 4,000 kg, comprising laser-guided ASMs, rockets, bombs, submunitions dispensers, incendiary tanks, guns and self-protection AAMs, while a twin-barrel GSh-2-30 30 mm cannon is mounted on the port fuselage.

In 1984, the more sophisticated anti-tank Su-25T first flew and evaluation aircraft were again tested in a conflict, this time in Chechnya. This was later developed as the Su-25TM, also known as the Su-39, first flown in 1996. The Su-25TM has a Kopyo-25 multi-mode radar and can use either a TV-optical system or FLIR for day or night capability respectively. Weapons load has been boosted to 6,000 kg with TV-guided ASMs, ARMs and radar-guided anti-ship missiles now potential weapons.

In 1987, production of the Su-25BM began, this aircraft using a more powerful and efficient 44.13 kN R-195 engine (also installed in the last of the earlier aircraft). The original Su-25SM programme, revealed in 1999, included a complete cockpit upgrade, increase in armament options and improvement in maintainability. The upgrade selected by the Russian air force, still termed Su-25SM, is much more limited, including a new fire-control computer and GPS capability. Russian aircraft are also to receive a pod-mounted Kopyo-25 radar and improved ECM capability.

Among non-Russian users, Peruvian aircraft have been involved in anti-drug operations. Georgia-based TAM and Elbit of Israel have developed the Scorpion/Su-25KM with cockpit modifications and armament expansion, the aircraft first flying in 2001. The Scorpion could use both Russian and Israeli weapons.

Specification (Su-25):
First flight: 22 February 1975
Current users: Armenia, Azerbaijan, Belarus (Su-25/UB), Bulgaria (Su-25A/UB), Georgia (Su-25/K/UB), Iraq (?), Kazakhstan, Macedonia (Su-25K/UB), Peru (Su-25/UB), Russia (Su-25/M/UB/Su-39), Slovakia (Su-25K/UBK), Turkmenistan, Ukraine and Uzbekistan. Includes aircraft used as trainers.
Crew: Pilot; two for trainer versions
Wing span: 14.36 m
Length: 15.53 m
Height: 4.80 m
Max take-off weight: 17,350 kg for early aircraft
Max weapon load: 4,000 kg
Maximum speed: Mach 0.82 (Mach 0.71 for early aircraft)
Service ceiling: 7,000 m
Maximum range: 500 km with maximum internal fuel at low altitude for early aircraft; 1,950 km with drop tanks for early aircraft

Su-25 being refuelled. Sergey Burdin

Sukhoi Su-30MKK/2/3 "Flanker"   Russia

One of the PLA Air Force's Su-30MKKs, prior to delivery. Hugo Mambour/AviaScribe

The Su-27 air superiority fighter has proven to be a suitable basis for the development of not only newer-generation fighters but also more attack-oriented aircraft. This is the case with the Su-30MKK series derived from the Su-30K fighter development of the Su-27. The Sukhoi Su-30MKK demonstrator first flew on 9 March 1999 almost a decade after the same aircraft made its maiden flight as the first prototype of the Su-30. The new type was developed and manufactured by KnAAPO specially for China and the Su-30MKK family represent that nation's most modern and capable strike force.

The airframe remains largely unchanged apart from overall strengthening to allow for the greater MTOW of 38,000 kg, increased by 7,500 kg from that of the Su-30K. Two of the same engines, the 122.59 kN-thrust with afterburning Lyulka-Saturn/Moscow AL-31F turbofan, are also used. Greater differences exist in systems fit, the radar being improved, a new glass cockpit installed and navigation, weapons control and EW equipment upgraded. The Su-30MKK2

has naval-optimised radar, M400 recce pod and Sapsan-E FLIR/EO and laser designation pod among other different systems. The Su-30MKK3 has the further improved N010M Zhuk-ME radar which can simultaneously detect 20 aerial targets and track and engage four of them or detect large warships at up to 200 km and simultaneously engage two. Systems introduced on the new variants could be retrofitted to earlier aircraft.

The Su-30MKK can carry an 8,000 kg payload on twelve stations. These could include R-27, R-73 and R-77 AAMs and Kh-29 laser/TV guided, Kh-31 anti-radiation and Kh-59M laser-guided ASMs and other LGBs, bombs and rockets while a further option is the Sapsan-E targeting pod. In addition to these weapons the Su-30MKK2 can employ the Kh-31A active-radar ASM. China ordered its first batch of aircraft in 1999 and subsequent re-orders have led to a total buy of at least 76. Deliveries to the PLAAF began in 2000. Su-30MKKs have been entering service with the PLAAF while Su-30MKK2s have joined the PLAN. Vietnam has ordered four Su-30MKKs.

Specification:
First flight: 9 March 1999 (Su-30MKK)
Current users: China, on order for Vietnam
Crew: Two
Wing span: 14.98 m with wingtip AAMs
Length: 21.94 m without probe
Height: 6.36 m
Empty weight: 17,900 kg
Max take-off weight: 38,000 kg
Max weapon load: 8,000 kg
Maximum speed: Mach 2
Service ceiling: 17,500 m
Maximum range: 1,500 km clean

Sukhoi Su-32/34 "Flanker"   **Russia**

The 'platypus'-nosed Su-32.
Colin Work

The Sukhoi Su-32 (also designated Su-34 and formerly Su-27IB) is a two-seat supersonic tactical strike aircraft that originated from a 1986 official Soviet requirement for an Su-27 attack derivative and the type is to replace the MiG-27, Su-17 and Su-24 and partially the Tu-22M in Russian service. The prototype T10V-1 first flew on 13 April 1990. Substantial re-design of the Su-27 airframe resulted in the side-by-side seating layout in the 'platypus' nose with the comfortable and spacious armour-plated cockpit notably offering good visibility.

The Su-32 is powered by a pair of 122.59 kN Lyulka-Saturn/Moscow AL-31F turbofans but the 175 kN AL-41F will equip future versions. In the summer of 1989 the aircraft set a number of world records. The passive phased-array radar can provide ground mapping to 150 km and track small targets to 30 km. It is complemented by an active radar installed in the tailboom for coverage aft of the aircraft. AAMs, possibly the R-74 will also be launched at such targets. 12 hardpoints allow the carriage of up to 8,000 kg of weapons and stores. These could include Kh-31P anti-radar, Kh-29T/L TV- and laser-guided ASMs and R-73 and R-77 AAMs. Su-32FN armament includes the Moskit anti-ship missile, Alpha ASM, Kh-59M TV-guided ASM, Kh-35 anti-ship missile and Kh-31 in addition to sonobuoys, ASW torpedoes and depth charges. The employment of satellite-guided munitions has also been

demonstrated. The Su-32FN maritime subtype with new radar and other avionics was revealed at the June 1995 Paris Air Show. An active stealth defence system has been evaluated on the Su-32. This generates a plasma cloud that surrounds the aircraft and blocks radar transmissions. Also under development are the Su-27R and Su-27PP, respectively dedicated armed reconnaissance and tactical EW aircraft.

Development of the costly Su-32 has been protracted and finding problems have meant that its service entry has been delayed to at least 2006, the first production standard aircraft flying on 20 December 2003. However more recently development has been accelerated, introducing this very capable machine into service now being considered a high priority of the Russian air force.

Specification:
First flight: 13 April 1990
Current users: Intended for Russia
Crew: Two
Wing span: 14.7 m
Length: 23.34 m without probe
Height: 6.08 m
Empty weight: 16,000 kg
Max take-off weight: 44,360 kg
Max weapon load: 8,000 kg
Maximum speed: 1,900 km/h
Maximum rate of climb: 18,000 metres/min
Maximum range: 600 km combat radius at low altitude, 4,000 kg weapons and internal fuel; 1,130 km for same conditions but with maximum fuel; 4,500 km ferry range

A Tu-22M on take-off. Paul Morley

Tupolev begun work on a VG strike platform in 1965 and the Tu-22M (NATO codename Backfire-A) first flew on 30 August 1969. The type, a medium range strategic bomber and missile launcher, is in fact the world's first VG bomber. The Tu-22M is a replacement for the Tu-16 and Tu-22

intermediate bombers for nuclear and conventional strike missions in Western Europe and China and against aircraft carriers and deliveries began to operational units in 1975. Development of the current Tu-22M3 also began that year with a first flight on 20 June 1977. In 1987-1989, Tu-22M2s were used in

the Afghan campaign. 1989 signified the Tu-22M3's (Backfire-C) formal induction into service.

The Tu-22M has a navigation/attack radar. The Tu-22M3 uses a pair of Kuznetsov NK-25 turbofans each of which produces 245.18 kN with afterburning. The aircraft has a

Tu-22M in flight with wings fully swept.
Paul Chandler

Another view of the Tu-22M.
Paul Morley

maximum payload of 24,000 kg but a more normal figure is 6,000 kg. Combat capability is claimed to be 2.2 times greater than that of the Tu-22M2.

Some 130 Tu-22M3s are in service with Russia, making it the country's numerically most important bomber. The Tu-22M was not exported but Ukraine inherited some and sixty remain in service. Some of Ukraine's Backfires are however being destroyed.

Tu-22M3s will receive a new radar and mission computer, avionics, EW and navigation systems and be renamed Tu-22M5. The radar will have improved terrain-following capability. Service life is also being extended to at least 2020. Another version is the reconnaissance Tu-22MR with a SLAR.

Specification: (Tu-22M3)
First flight: 30 August 1969 (Tu-22M)
Current users: Russia and Ukraine
Crew: Four
Wing span: 34.28 m spread; 23.3 m swept
Length: 42.46 m
Height: 11.05 m
Empty weight: 52,000 kg
Max take-off weight: 124,000 kg
Max weapon load: 24,000 kg
Maximum speed: Mach 1.8
Service ceiling: 14,000 m
Maximum range: 2,200 km radius at high altitude, some supersonic flight, with one Kh-22

A Tu-95 about to land.
Keith Blincow

The majestic Tu-95, called Bear by NATO, uniquely marries turboprop engines to a swept wing to just as uniquely allow both high speed (just under Mach 0.9) and long range (17,500 km) flight. First flying on 12 November 1952, this strategic bomber has outlasted jet-powered competitors and is still an important member of the Soviet bomber triad. Versions were also produced for maritime, reconnaissance and ELINT.

The current Tu-95MS (Bear-H) version flew in 1979 and entered service in 1984. In-service subtypes are Tu-95MS6 and Tu-95MS16. The Tu-95MS6/16, despite their name, were derived from the Tu-142 ASW version of the Tu-95.

The Tu-95 has a nose-mounted main radar with a weather radar above it. The Tu-95 has an aircrew of seven, a tail-gunner being retained. The aircraft is driven by four Samara/Kuznetsov NK-12MP turboprops, each capable of 11,185 ekW. A maximum 20,000kg of weapons can be carried. These include the Kh-55 cruise missile in the centre-fuselage bomb bay for the older Tu-95MS6 or the Kh-55SM in the fuselage and under the wing of the Tu-95MS16. Aircraft will be updated to use the Kh-101.

Russia now has three regiments with the aircraft, its fleet being boosted by

Front view of the Tu-95. Ian Powell

The Tu-95 is finished in a bare-metal colour scheme. Keith Blincow

aircraft from Kazakhstan and the Ukraine. Russia's aircraft have been updated to use the Kh-101 and Kh-555 conventional long-range missiles.

Navigation and defensive capabilities are also improved and airframe life extended. Tu-95 service life is being extended for operations to 2010 but with no replacement type in sight, the aircraft will probably remain in service well after that date.

Specification: (Tu-95MS)
First flight: 12 November 1952 (Tu-95)
Current users: Russia
Crew: Seven
Wing span: 50.04 m
Length: 49.13 m
Height: 13.30 m
Empty weight: 94,400 kg
Max take-off weight: 185,000 kg
Max weapon load: 20,000 kg
Maximum speed: 830 km/h
Service ceiling: 10,500 m
Maximum range: 10,500 km with normal combat load

The Tupolev Tu-160 (NATO codename Blackjack) is a supersonic strategic bomber, the only such type in service with the Russian Air Force. It was developed in response to a 1970 Soviet requirement for an aircraft capable of 2,000 km/h, with a maximum range of 14,000-16,000km, these parameters being downgraded from a 1967 specification. The Tu-160, based on the Tu-144 airliner, was selected over the rival Myasischev M-18 design. The 70-01 prototype made its maiden flight on 19 December 1981, the first production example flying in 1984.

The aircraft features wing-body blending with wing leading edge root extensions (LERX). Avionics include the main radar and TFR. The Tu-160 is powered by four Samara NK-321 turbofans, each of which produces 245.18 kN with afterburning. The

"Gromov", one of Russia's Tu-160s, which are all named after legendary national figures.
Hugo Mambour/AviaScribe

aircraft can fly for fifteen hours without air-to-air refuelling. The crew numbers four. In 1989/90 the Tu-160 claimed forty-four flight records.

Theoretical total payload is 45,000 kg. Weapons used include the Kh-

A Tu-160 cleans up after take-off.
Hugo Mambour/AviaScribe

55SM cruise, the non-nuclear Kh-555 variant or the Kh-15 shorter-range missile and eventually the long-range Kh-101 and medium-range Kh-SD; the conventional capability is now being given more emphasis and is a major focus of proposed upgrades. Still unlike on the US's B-1 and B-2 strategic bombers, free-fall bombs are not employed on the Tu-160.

The Russian Air Force fleet numbers fourteen, eight being received from the Ukraine, and these are based at Engels in central Russia. The service aims for a total of twenty-five aircraft. In 1997 the production line was re-opened, the first new-build aircraft entering operational service in 2000. The Ukraine has a smaller force.

Funding shortages have meant that the Russian aircraft have been poorly maintained. Still, by 2004 the Kazan Aviation Production Association will have installed upgraded avionics in the Tu-160 fleet while the aircraft are subsequently also due to undergo a more comprehensive avionics modernization. Versions have been suggested for reconnaissance and

ECM escort.

Specification:
First flight: 19 December 1981
Current users: Russia
Crew: Four
Wing span: 35.6 m spread; 55.7 m swept
Length: 54.1 m
Height: 13.1 m
Empty weight: 117,000 kg
Max take-off weight: 275,000 kg
Max weapon load: 45,000 kg
Maximum speed: Mach 2.05
Service ceiling: 15,600 m
Maximum range: 2,000 km combat radius at Mach 1.5; 12,300 km range at Mach 0.77 with six Kh-55 dropped mid-range and 5% fuel reserve

Head-on view of the Tu-160. Hugo Mambour/AviaScribe

UTVA J-22 Orao   Serbia/Romania

In 1970 Yugoslavia and Romania agreed to the YUROM collaborative programme to develop a twin-engined transonic aircraft for CAS, battlefield air interdiction, reconnaissance and limited air defence, the primary contractors then being Soko and CNIAR respectively. The resulting aircraft was produced as the J-22 Orao in Yugoslavia and IAR-93 in Romania. The Yugoslav and Romanian single-seat prototypes made their maiden flights on 31 October 1974. The corresponding two-seat aircraft first flew on 29 January 1977. Production began in Romania in 1979 and in Yugoslavia the following year.

IAR-93A, the first Romanian model, was followed by the IAR-93B which flew in 1985 and which has a payload increased to the figure below. Soko-produced pre-production aircraft, which entered service, are the single-seat IJ-22, used for reconnaissance, and the two-seat INJ-22A. The J-22A Orao I, the counterpart of the IAR-93A, has an improved weapons load. The single-seat J-22B Orao II, comparable to the IAR-93B, introduced the afterburning engine. The NJ-22 was the two-seat version.

One under-fuselage and four-underwing hardpoints enable the carriage of 2,800 kg of stores (although only 1,500 kg for the IAR-93A). Air-to-ground weapons include free fall, retarded, cluster, fragmentation or incendiary bombs, laser-guided, anti-radar and anti-ship missiles (including Maverick and Grom). IR-guided AAMs could be carried including on the wingtips. There is also a pair of twin-barrel GS-23L 23 mm cannons mounted at the engine inlets. The J-22B uses two 22.24 kN (with afterburning) Orao/Turbomecanica (Rolls-Royce/Bristol Siddeley) Viper Mk 633-41 turbojets. Romanian aircraft are in storage but Serbia and Republika Sprska still fly the type.

Specification: (Orao II)
First flight: 31 October 1974
Current users: Republika Sprska and Serbia
Crew: Pilot (J-22); two (NJ-22)
Wing span: 9.62 m
Length: 14.9 m (single-seater, with probe)
Height: 4.45 m
Empty weight: 5,700 kg
Max take-off weight: 11,200 kg
Max weapon load: 2,800 kg
Maximum speed: 1,160 km/h
Maximum rate of climb: 4,500 metres/min at sea level
Service ceiling: 13,500 m
Maximum range: 530 km at high altitude with maximum external load

Orao on display with stores.
Salinger Igor

Xian H-6 (B-6) "Badger"   China

In 1957, China was granted a licence to locally manufacture the Tupolev Tu-16 medium-range strategic bomber, the first Chinese-assembled aircraft, known as the H-6, flying two years later. Harbin undertook early work on the H-6, but in the early 1960s responsibility for the type was transferred to Xian. However, the break in Chinese-Soviet relations around that time slowed the progress of the Chinese efforts. The first fully indigenous H-6 derivative, the H-6A (B-6A) made its maiden flight on 24 December 1968. Power was provided by a pair of 93.16 kN Xian WP-8 (Mikulin AM-3) turbojets.

The H-6A could be armed with bombs, missiles and torpedoes and in

The H-6 bomber. Ruud Leeuw

particular it also had a nuclear capability, total payload being 9,000 kg. The type was further improved as the H-6D (B-6D) which had new and upgraded avionics. This aircraft, which first flew in 1981, was one of the first Chinese aircraft to employ air-to-surface missiles against warships, with a pair of C-101 (YJ-6) and more recently the C-611 (YJ-6I) missiles

being standard armament. A nuclear-optimised model of the H-6 was also developed. The H-6E/F (B-6E/F) has improved bombing, navigation and ECM/ESM equipment but the ultimate EW version is the H-6D.

PLAN H-6s could be armed with cruise missiles and additionally some PLAAF aircraft are also being fitted to carry such weapons. China further has been evaluating the use of a new land attack cruise missile on the aircraft. Video released in 2002 showed four such weapons on the underwing pylons of a new version of the aircraft, the H-6H developed from the H-6D.

In 1998, an initial batch of H-6s underwent conversion into H-6U (B-6U) air-to-air refuelling tankers configured with a pair of hose- and drogue-pods. This model was first revealed in October 1999. China's first tanker, the H-6Us support J-8 and other tactical fighter operations. H-6Ds are also being given an aerial refuelling capability.

Up to 150 H-6s are in service with the PLAAF and PLAN. China requires a replacement for this obsolete aircraft, particularly since Russia has refused to sell it the Tu-22M3.

Specification:
First flight: 24 December 1968
Current users: China
Crew: Six
Wing span: 34.19 m
Length: 34.8 m
Height: 9.85 m
Max take-off weight: 75,800 kg
Max weapon load: 9,000 kg
Maximum speed: 1,014 km/h at 6,250 m
Maximum range: 4,300 km with full fuel

Xian JH-7 Flying Leopard China

A JH-7 about to land. via Timothy Yan

With the need to replace the obsolescent H-5 in the maritime attack role and the failure to suitably evolve the Q-5 for that mission, China in the mid-early 1970s took the ambitious step to develop what would eventually become its first indigenous production combat aircraft. This design emerged as a two-seat, twin-engined, all-weather day/night-capable strike aircraft in the class of the Tornado or Su-24. The JH-7 (fighter-bomber-7) Flying Leopard first flew on 14 December 1988, as the H-7, but the type was only publicly revealed in 1996.

By 1994, the JH-7 was entering service to fulfil a naval requirement believed to be for seventy-two aircraft but only twenty are estimated to have been produced so far, most if not all for test and evaluation.

In 1975, the Chinese signed with Rolls Royce to co-produce the Rolls-Royce Spey 202 turbofan engine which produces 91.26 kN of thrust with afterburning, although problems have since been encountered in its local production and further examples are reported to have been imported. Systems fit is improved in the export

FBC-1 and includes the JL-10 Shen Ying multi-mode pulse-Doppler radar replacing the JH-7's Type 232H Eagle Eye, and the use of new navigation and FLIR/laser-targeting pods, cockpit displays and helmet-mounted sighting systems. Some of these devices may also be installed in the JH-7. The more advanced JH-7A is a glass cockpit-equipped FBW machine that will be powered by local Xian WS-9 versions of the Spey. An EW/ECR version has also been mooted.

The aircraft has been found to be underpowered and its weapons load is small for its class.

Four or six hardpoints under the wings, depending on the model, and one under the fuselage allow the carriage of free-fall bombs or the C-701, C-801 (YJ-8) and C-802K (YJ-8K) anti-ship missiles. Another possible weapon is the Kh-31P (YJ-91) anti-radiation anti-ship missile. Wingtip pylons can accommodate short-ranged AAMs. The JH-7 has a twin-barrel 23 mm cannon installed under the starboard fuselage.

Unlike Russian designs in Chinese service, the JH-7 could use locally developed weapons in particular the C-801/802. However the aircraft has had a long gestation period and the capability of the type is far exceeded by that of the Su-30MKK/2/3 now entering PLAAF/PLAN service.

Specification:
First flight: 14 December 1988
Current users: China
Crew: Two
Wing span: 12.71 m
Length: 22.33 m with probe
Height: 6.58 m
Max take-off weight: 28,475 kg
Max weapon load: 6,500 kg
Maximum speed: Mach 1.7
Service ceiling: 15,600 m
Maximum range: 900-1,650 km combat radius; 3,650 km range with full internal fuel and no weapons

Glossary

AESA	Active electronically scanned array		FAC	Forward air control
AAM	Air-to-air missile		FBW	Fly-by-wire
AdA	Armée de l'Air (French Air Force)		FLIR	Forward-looking infrared
ALARM	Air-launched anti-radiation missile		FOAS	Future offensive air system
ALCM	Air-launched cruise missile		FOC	Full operational capability
AMI	Aeronautica Militare Italiano (Italian Air Force)			
ARM	Anti-radiation missile		GPS	Global Positioning System
ASM	Air-to-surface missile		GP	General Purpose
ASMP	Air-Sol Moyenne Portée			
			HARM	High-speed Anti-Radiation Missile
BLOS	Beyond-line-of-sight		HOTAS	Hands-on-throttle-and-stick
BVR	Beyond visual range		HUD	Heads-up-display
CAS	Close air support		IAF	Indian Air Force
CV	Carrier-borne		INU	Inertial navigation unit
CM	Cruise missile		INS	Inertial navigation system
COIN	Counter-insurgency		IFF	Identification-friend-or-foe
CTOL	Conventional take-off and landing		IOC	Initial operational capability
			IPGM	Improved Precision Guided-Bomb
ECM	Electronic countermeasure		IR	Infrared
ECR	Electronic combat and reconnaissance			
EO	Electro-optical		JASDF	Japanese Air Self-Defence Force
EW	Electronic warfare		JASSM	Joint Air-to-Surface Standoff Missile
			JATO	Jet-assisted take-off
126 FA	Frontal aviation (of Soviet/Russian air forces)		JDAM	Joint Direct Attack Munition

JTIDS	Joint Tactical Information Distribution System	SAM	Surface-to-air missile
JSF	Joint Strike Fighter	SDB	Small Diameter Bomb
JSOW	Joint standoff weapon	SEAD	Suppression of enemy air defences
		STOVL	Short take-off and vertical landing
LGB	Laser-guided bomb		
		TAC	(US Air Force) Tactical Air Command
MFD	Multi-function display	TIALD	Thermal Imaging Airborne Laser Designation
MIDS	Multifunction Information Distribution System	TFR	Terrain following radar
MLU	Mid-life update		
MTOW	Maximum take-off weight	UN	United Nations
		USAF	US Air Force
NATO	North Atlantic Treaty Organization	USMC	US Marine Corps
NVG	Night vision goggles	USN	US Navy
PGB	Precision guided bomb	VG	Variable geometry
PLAN	(Chinese) People's Liberation Army Navy	V/STOL	Vertical/short take-off and landing
PLAAF	(Chinese) People's Liberation Army Air Force		
		WCMD	Wind-Corrected Munitions Dispenser
RAF	Royal Air Force		
RAAF	Royal Australian Air Force		
RHAWS	Radar homing and warning system		
RWR	Radar warning receiver		
SAAF	South African Air Force		
SAC	(US Air Force) Strategic Air Command		

Picture Credits

The author and publisher would like to thank the following individuals and organizations for the supply of photos: Mariusz Adamski (Su-22). Alenia Aeronautica (AMX x3). Abbas Ali (A-5). BAE SYSTEMS (Tornado, FOAS artist impression). Sven de Bevere (F-15E, Alpha Jet A). Keith Blincow (B-52H, F-15I, Tu-95 x2). Sergey Burdin (Su-25 x2). Damien Burke (Jaguar x2). George Canciani (B-1B, A-4SU). Paul Chandler (Tu-22M). Chilean Air Force (A-37B, A-36). Dassault Aviation (Mirage 2000N, Mirage 2000D, Jaguar). EADS (Tornado x3). EMBRAER (Super Tucano). Rafael Finter (Mirage 2000D). Erik Frikke (OV-10). Salinger Igor (Jastreb, Orao). Olaf Juergensmeier (A-7). Lawrence Livermore National Laboratory (Hypersoar artist's impression). Ruud Leeuw (H-6). Lockheed Martin (T-50 artist's impression, FB-22 artist's impression, X-35A x2, F-117A, Mitsubishi F-2). Hugo Mambour/AviaScribe (H-5, Su-24M x3, Su-25TM, Su-30MKK, Tu-160 x3). Neil C Martin (MiG-17). Alastair McBean (F-111). Paul Morley (Tu-22M x2). Colin Norwood (Super Etendard). Gerhard Plomitzer (B-2A). Ian Powell (Tu-95). Anders Presterud (MB-339PAN). Royal Air Force/Crown Copyright (Harrier x3). US Air Force, B-1B x2, B-2, B-52 x2, F-15E, AC-130, F-117A x2, A-10A x3, B-2A x2). US Marine Corps (X-35B). Rogier Westerhuis/Aero Image (Pucara, MiG-27). Colin Work (Su-32). World Airnews (Impala Mk.2). via Timothy Yan (JH-7). Jaroslaw Zaczek (Mitsubishi F-1)

The author and publisher would also like to thank Johan Lundgren/ Airliners.net for providing photographic assistance.